T0095224

Rising Above It All

Rising Above It All

The art of living a more fulfilling and productive life

John L. Lee

RISING ABOVE IT ALL
THE ART OF LIVING A MORE FULFILLING AND PRODUCTIVE LIFE

iUniverse books may be ordered through booksellers or by contacting:

iUniverse
1663 Liberty Drive
Bloomington, IN 47403
www.iuniverse.com
1-800-Authors (1-800-288-4677)

Because of the dynamic nature of the Internet, any web addresses or links contained in this book may have changed since publication and may no longer be valid. The views expressed in this work are solely those of the author and do not necessarily reflect the views of the publisher, and the publisher hereby disclaims any responsibility for them.

Any people depicted in stock imagery provided by Thinkstock are models, and such images are being used for illustrative purposes only.
Certain stock imagery © Thinkstock.

ISBN: 978-1-4917-7771-8 (sc)
ISBN: 978-1-4917-7773-2 (hc)
ISBN: 978-1-4917-7772-5 (e)

Library of Congress Control Number: 2015915991

Print information available on the last page.

iUniverse rev. date: 11/20/2017

This book is dedicated to the following people:

My parents,
Jim and Edna Lee,
whose sacrifices for their children literally wore them out.
I will never be able to repay you.
Thanks!

My lovely wife, whom I deeply love,
Rita.

My children, who are the pride of my life,
Craig, Chad, Brian, and Jason.

My grandchildren,
for whom I wrote this book.

Contents

Introduction

Dear reader, I want you to know what an honor it has been for me to write this book. I hope that you will feel as inspired reading it as I felt writing it. The objective of this work is to inspire you to live a more fulfilling and productive life.

The writing of this book was not a natural act for me, and I could not have completed such an act without the patient help of my chief editor and friend Dorothy Openshaw. The reason I took on this challenge is really quite simple—I just want to make a difference. When I started lecturing on the way I viewed life and business, I realized that it inspired people. Many people told me that my simple lecture changed their lives. They asked me to write a book, and so I did. In short, the target audience for this book is you. I hope it inspires you to create a more fulfilling and productive life so we can improve upon the human condition. I truly believe that we are in the dark ages of our human potential. I hope to teach you how to rise above these dark ages into a new and more enlightened understanding of what we call life. Only you, the reader, can judge my success or lack thereof.

I believe that one important element of living a more fulfilling and productive life is to understand the beauty of human nature. Many books have been written on the vices and deviant nature of human beings, but seldom has a book been written on the purpose, depth, beauty, and nature of human potential.

Ultimately, my hope is that you, the reader, will be inspired by your newfound knowledge and go out and make the world a better place for the people and organizations you serve.

Chapter One

The Art of Fulfillment

Through my own life experiences, I have come to realize that people are social creatures, and if we are to experience higher levels of fulfillment, we need to feel that we belong and that we contribute to something worthwhile.

Knowledge and understanding are very important elements in creating a more fulfilling and productive life. Knowledge and understanding have the potential of ultimately creating purpose. If there is no purpose in your life, then you will not find fulfillment or feel productive. With that being said, I will begin this study by teaching you the nature of human nature.

Throughout this discussion, I will refer back to two rules of human fulfillment:

1. You will never become greater than that which motivates you.
2. You stop becoming greater the instant you think you're great.

Throughout this discussion, we will also investigate the importance of providing leadership. For this discussion, leadership is defined as the ability to change culture. Culture is often referred to as an organization's personality. Organization can refer to many different entities, including a business or a family. That being said, let's begin. I have identified three levels of human behavior: phase 1 behavior, phase 2 behavior, and phase 3 behavior.

This model uses two basic assumptions concerning human nature. The first assumption is that the mother of all motivators is survival. Like all living creatures, we humans do amazing things just to survive. There is a program on television called *Survival Stories* that goes over the amazing things people do just to survive. A few years ago, there was an individual who was rock climbing in the state of Utah when a rock fell on his forearm. As a result of this misfortune, he was pinned under that rock for three or four days. When he felt he wasn't going to survive much longer, he finally took out his pocketknife and cut off his arm. He then managed to hike out to get help. That shows how strong a motivator survival is. Remember—the first assumption is that the mother of all motivators is survival.

The second assumption is that if people do not perceive that they stand out in a crowd, they will die. Using these two assumptions, I will attempt to explain human nature.

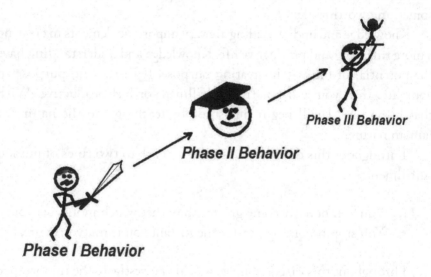

Phase III Behavior

Phase II Behavior

Phase I Behavior

As you can see, there are three levels of human behavior—phases I, 2, and 3. The model will be symbolized as shown in the illustration above. Phase I behavior is symbolized by an individual holding a sword, phase 2 behavior is symbolized by an individual with a graduation cap, and phase 3 is symbolized by an individual lifting someone up.

Phase I Behavior

Phase I behavior is the starting point of human behavior. In an effort to survive, we engage in phase I behavior that tears other people down— as a way to help us perceive that we are standing out in a crowd. If we cut everyone down around us, then, relatively speaking, we will be standing out in a crowd—it's all relative. For example, what happens to a child who goes to school and is different in some way? Phase I behavior identifies unique characteristics, magnifies them, and belittles them. Imagine the shock of a child who has been taught that his uniqueness makes him special and then goes to school, where his uniqueness is amplified and belittled by other students. The child then comes home believing that the message that his uniqueness makes him special is nothing but a big lie and that in reality his uniqueness only qualifies him as some kind of a freak show. That's what phase I behavior does—it amplifies uniqueness and then belittles it. Phase I organizations tend to gravitate to the center. People try to be the same so no one will belittle them. Uniqueness is seen as a liability in a phase I organization.

An important thing to understand here is that phase I behavior doesn't just take bad characteristics and belittle them. It doesn't matter if the characteristic is positive or negative; it just needs to be a unique characteristic. I've heard of children who went to school and were teased and belittled because they got good grades. Then they would purposely get bad grades just so they could belong to the crowd. That's the nature of phase I behavior.

To continue on with the story, the child in question usually comes home crying, and the mother responds by asking, "How can children be so mean?"

Phase I behavior, by its very nature, tends to be insecure, and thus the starting point of human nature tends to believe the critics. Critics are very powerful in a phase I environment because everyone cares what others think of him. For example, when the child goes to school and the other kids say he's a freak because he gets good grades, he tends to believe them because human nature tends to believe the critics in phase I. This belief that the critics are right is what gives phase I behavior the power to do negative things, especially if it happens within a phase I organization that values and supports this type of behavior. Phase I behavior is also the birthplace of practices such as racism, sexism, and other destructive behaviors.

Phase I behavior will attempt to keep people from evolving out of this lower level of behavior and attempts to convince people that they are incapable of improving. Phase I behavior is inherently destructive. Thus, phase I behavior is inherently incapable of creating an environment of fulfillment and productivity. People who exhibit phase I behavior are incapable of becoming leaders in the world of organizational change, at least change for the good. I will be referring to this organizational change for the good as organizational transformation. The definition of leadership in the world of organizational transformation is the ability to change culture for the good. Culture is defined as how an organization acts out on its value system and is also referred to as the personality of an organization. Organizational culture is very difficult to change. A leader must be very influential in order to change organizational culture. Phase I behavior is not influential for the good and as a result is incapable of true leadership.

• Phase I behavior is often referred to as the cheap drug of human behavior

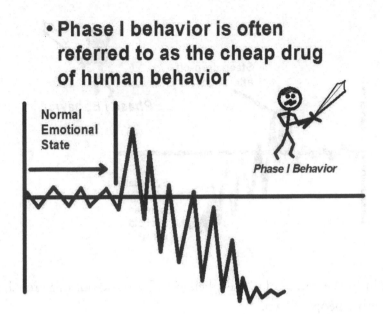

Normal Emotional State

Phase I Behavior

Phase I behavior is the cheap drug of human behavior. Let me describe the nature of this cheap drug. I'll begin by describing the normal emotional state of a human being. A person's emotional state goes up and down within a reasonable amount of variation. When the lower side of this reasonable amount of variation in emotional state has been reached, a person may desire to have a "high," so a choice is made to take the cheap drug. This drug does give people the high they are looking for. Of course, the nature of the cheap drug is that after experiencing the high, then the steep drop-off is experienced. Now the desire is to experience a high again because now that person is lower than the original state. So the person takes another hit, and the cheap drug results in another high. However, the nature of the drug is that the new high is lower than the last high. This cycle continues until eventually each new high is lower than the old norm.

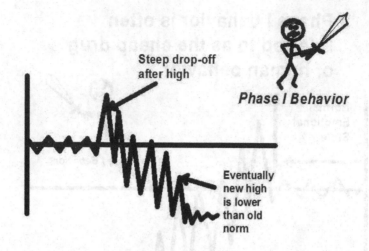

Steep drop-off after high

Phase I Behavior

Eventually new high is lower than old norm

This is the nature of phase I behavior. To stand out in a crowd, you chop other people down.

Phase I Behavior is the starting point of human behavior but it should not be the ending point of human behavior.

Remember that phase I behavior is the starting point of human behavior. If you decide to habitually practice phase I behavior, your reward will be jealousy, enviousness, and hatefulness. You will be easily offended, and you will experience a lack of influence for good. These are the fruits of phase I behavior. In hindsight, phase I behavior will always look stupid and shameful.

Every phase of behavior has its own decision-making processes, as well as its own set of motives. Phase I behavior solves problems with the personify, blame, and punish (PBP) methodology. With phase I behavior, every problem is a personal problem and every personal problem is solved through effective punishment. Effective punishment, or PBP, has the natural by-product of fear. Remember that you'll never become greater than that which motivates you, and phase I behavior is motivated by fear. This behavior also lacks the influence that is required to evolve to higher levels of fulfillment.

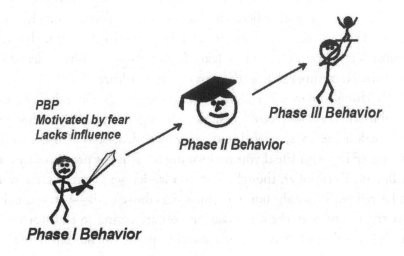

PBP
Motivated by fear
Lacks influence

Phase III Behavior

Phase II Behavior

Phase I Behavior

In the figure above I have upgraded our model on human behavior by adding a few bullet points about phase I behavior.

I have been a plant manager for several companies, and sometimes I would go into an organization that had just been purchased by an unfriendly takeover or something similar. I'd notice that these organizations were very much phase I organizations. In my rookie season, I initially thought that if I was nice to everyone, then eventually they would be nice in return. Wrong! In reality, that never happened. I quickly learned that phase I behavior respects fear, so I changed my style.

I would go into these organizations and say, "Hey, listen. You may not like me, and I don't blame you, but the fact of the matter is I am your boss and I have rules." And then I stated the rules. I would say, "If you disobey the rules, I want you to know that I will terminate you immediately." And so they feared me—and that was when I suddenly realized that phase I behavior–type organizations respect fear; therefore, they respected my position. Remember that you cannot lead if you do not have the respect of the organization you're trying to lead and phase I behavior is motivated by fear.

Obviously, this is not where you want to keep the organization. Your job in a leadership role is to evolve the organization to higher levels of human behavior. But this is a starting point, and you do have to deal with reality. Reality doesn't care what you wish the organization was or is; you have to deal with where you currently are. You ultimately want to evolve the organization from phase I behavior to the point that the organization is not motivated by fear. This change in culture demands leadership. Remember that leadership dictates culture.

One thing to remember is that one of the things that takes place if you habitually exercise phase I behavior throughout your life is that you will be jealous, envious, hateful, and easily offended. Phase I is not where you want to live your life if you are looking for a life of productivity and fulfillment. Remember, though, that as a leader, you cannot effectively beat hatred with hatred; thus, you must rise above it all—you must rise above the behavior of the organization you are trying to transform. So even though phase I behavior is a starting point for human nature, it does not have to be the ending condition. The good news is that human nature is capable of evolving. Evolving to higher levels of human behavior usually demands help from those who have matured and progressed out of phase I behavior. Evolution also demands personal courage, strength, and a belief that the seemingly impossible is possible and obtainable. In other words, you must be capable of going against the critics.

In summary, phase I behavior is good at creating problems but dysfunctional at solving them, which is another way of saying it is a destructive behavior.

Chapter Two

Phase 2 Behavior

Phase 2 behavior is when you develop skills and talents that allow you to stand out in a crowd. As you develop skills and talents, you have less of a desire to use phase I behavior to stand out. You may wonder why this is the case. The reason is because the high you get from standing out in a crowd based on skills and talents is a higher, more sustainable high than the one you would get from phase I behavior. Phase 2 behavior does not have the same steep drop-offs as the cheap drug of phase I human behavior. Ultimately, you evolve out of lower levels to higher levels of human behavior simply because it feels better. It's actually pretty basic.

Evolving to higher levels of human behavior usually demands help from those that have matured out of Phase I behavior.

Phase II Behavior

It also demands personal courage, strength, and a belief that the seemingly impossible is possible and doable (proving critics wrong).

Phase I Behavior

Phase 2 behavior is relatively constructive, so that's a good thing. We can develop skills and talents through formal education or informal education, which is symbolized by the graduation cap. But however they are learned, we have to develop skills and talents to evolve to phase 2 behavior.

When this model was being realized in my mind, I was a father of four relatively young boys. At the time, my eldest son was in second grade, and the youngest was a toddler. Through observation, I noticed phase I behavior developing in my children. Therefore, I decided I would try introducing them to the joys of higher-level human behavior, such as phase 2 behavior. I felt I needed to find a lonely person for my kids to stand out in a crowd with based on their limited skills and talents.

One evening after work I dropped by the local elder-care facility. I went up to the lady at the front desk and asked her, "Is there anyone in this facility who is extremely lonely?" She responded without hesitation and told me about Mary. Mary had not had a visitor in twelve years. I quickly told the lady at the front desk that she would be perfect. I then left the facility, went home, and told my wife about Mary and how I felt it would be a good opportunity for the boys to experience the joys of serving others by using their skills and talents. I figured Mary was so lonely that the slightest amount of talent could pull this one off. My wife agreed and immediately started working on the project by teaching the kids some new songs.

Within a couple of weeks, she had the kids perform their dress rehearsal. I felt that they did an excellent job. After a little polishing of the production, my wife informed me that they were ready for the big performance, so one Sunday afternoon we got the kids dressed up in their cute little outfits and headed out to the care center.

We arrived at the front desk and announced to the attendant that we had come to see Mary. She was shocked that someone had actually come to visit Mary. She happily led us back to Mary's room. When we arrived, there she was in a deep sleep. I told the young lady not to wake her up and that we could come back later.

The lady quickly responded, "Are you kidding me, sir? This wonderful woman has not had a visitor for twelve years. Do you really think I'm going to let you escape?"

I couldn't really think of a counterargument, so we stayed.

With the persuasive efforts of the young lady, Mary eventually woke up. The attendant told her, "Mary, you have company."

I could tell by the look on her face that Mary was shocked. Mary informed us that she needed to get ready and made me promise that we would not leave. I gave her my promise and left her room. While my young family was waiting outside the room, I rubbed my hands together and told them that Mary was on her way. After we waited for ten or fifteen minutes, Mary walked out of her room dressed in what I perceived to be her best clothing. She had a warm smile on her face as she sat down, and my wife started asking her questions about herself.

Mary started talking, and an hour flew by—and then she stopped and asked us about the children. This is where their practice was to kick in. So I brought the children forward, straightened up their clothing, and reminded them of what they had practiced. To my relief, the kids performed as planned. Each child went up to Mary, looked her right in the face, and introduced himself. Then my wife announced to Mary that the kids had prepared some songs they wanted to sing to her. My wife brushed each of the kids down and had them all line up in front of Mary; then they started singing. They were doing a great job. *Wow, those genes must have come from their mother!* I thought. Soon I noticed tears building up in the corners of Mary's eyes. The next thing I knew, tears were flowing freely down her face.

I thought to myself, *This is exactly what the kids needed.* When the first song was over, Mary asked if they could sing another song. My wife informed her that the kids had practiced four songs and that they desired to share all of them with her. By the time they had finished all four songs, my wife and Mary were openly crying.

At the end of the fourth song, I watched my children observing their mom and Mary. I gave my sons high fives for the great performance, and my eldest son looked at me and said, "I think we did a good job."

I told all the boys that they had just done an excellent job. I asked them, "Do you feel good?" They all responded in the affirmative. I could tell that the boys had just learned how to stand out in a crowd based on their skills and talents. The exercise was a success.

Eventually, all the boys went up and gave Mary a hug, and we began to leave. As I looked around, I was surprised at the impact this performance had had on everyone around us. It seemed everyone was in tears. As we exited the building through the various hallways, I noticed that at the corners of the hallways were various nurses, and all of them had red and puffed-up eyes from the emotional experience. I must admit that I was greatly surprised at the influence this small act had on all those people. At that moment, I started to realize the power of this kind of behavior.

In Phase II behavior we learn to stand out in a crowd by developing our skills and talents.

Phase II behavior does not have the nasty after taste of Phase I behavior.

Phase II Behavior

In phase 2 behavior, we learn to stand out in a crowd by both developing our skills and talents and then exercising them in society. Phase 2 behavior does not have the nasty aftertaste of phase I behavior.

From our experience with Mary, I can tell you that my sons felt good to stand out in a crowd based on their skills and talents. My sons exercised their skills and talents, and *wow*, they really stood out in the crowd! I noticed that they recognized this and found this to be something good. It was my hope, as a father, that they would start to practice this form of behavior to stand out in a crowd and divorce themselves from phase I behavior.

I wish I could tell you as a parent that you only need to do something like this once, but I've learned—not only in teaching children but in teaching anyone—that redundancy is a powerful and necessary tool. Obviously, you don't just do this once for your organization either. You give people many opportunities over and over to stand out in a crowd based on their skills and talents.

As I previously said, individuals desire phase 2 behavior over phase 1 behavior because it naturally feels better. The good feelings from phase 2 behavior are a powerful motivator, and people will dedicate their lives to improving skills and talents so that they can spend more time in it.

However, phase 2 behavior does still have some of the stains of phase 1 behavior. The relationship between the two behaviors is that a person with phase 2 behavior secretly desires others to fail if they are developing the same skills and talents that he has and currently uses to stand out in a crowd. But what makes phase 2 different from phase 1 is that phase 1 wants everyone to fail. Phase 2 behavior finds those with the same skills and talents to be threatening to their ability to stand out in a crowd; thus, it threatens their very survival. Symbolically speaking, when no one is looking, phase 2 behavior will throw out the proverbial banana peel and hope the "competition" slips.

Phase 2 behavior respects skills and talents, and because of this, phase 2 organizations will allow you to lead them as long as they perceive you have more skills and talents than they have. Organizations will not allow you to lead them unless they respect you. As soon as phase 2 people perceive that they have more skill and talent than their leaders, they will lose respect for them and will not allow themselves to be led by them. In other words, once phase 2 people perceive that they have more skill and talent than their boss, they will attempt to undermine the boss's authority.

Phase 2 behavior seeks self-glorification. Therefore, when a phase 2 behavior person does something good, he desires to share it with others in an effort to bring attention to himself. What people are doing here is trying to stand out in a crowd based on their skills and talents so that they bring attention to themselves (self-glorification). Phase 2 behavior is relatively constructive and is a big improvement over phase 1. Because people with phase 2 behavior expend a great deal of energy letting as many people as possible know of their skills, talents, and good works, a natural by-product of phase 2 behavior can be to make other people feel inadequate in their presence.

Phase 2 behavior may even realize that the feeling of stupidity exists, because the main priority of people with phase 2 behavior is to make themselves stand out in a crowd based on their skills and talents. As a result, they will not compromise this value of skills and talents to compensate for the perceived insecurities of another.

In summary, phase 2 behavior is a constructive behavior that respects skills and talents and desires to be recognized for the social benefits that are achieved during the implementation of those skills and talents. An organization can go a long way on phase 2 behavior.

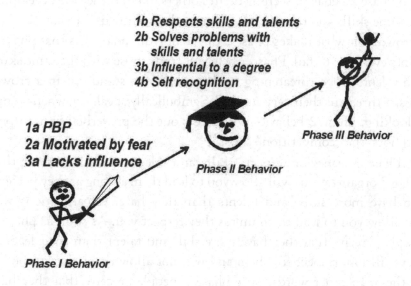

1b Respects skills and talents
2b Solves problems with skills and talents
3b Influential to a degree
4b Self recognition

1a PBP
2a Motivated by fear
3a Lacks influence

Phase III Behavior

Phase II Behavior

Phase I Behavior

I have again upgraded the information in the model on human nature. Notice that it says: respects skills and talents, solves problems with skills and talents, influential to a degree, and self-recognition. Eventually, human nature has the potential to master phase 2 behavior to the extent that this former behavior becomes boring and unfulfilling. When this is experienced, then human nature is capable of evolving to phase 3 behavior.

Chapter Three

Phase 3 Behavior

Phase 3 behavior is the crowning achievement of human behavior, because the key phrase for phase 3 behavior is "to lift up." Phase 3 behavior can only be realized after overcoming phase 1 behavior and mastering phase 2 behavior. You cannot evolve from phase 1 behavior straight to phase 3 behavior. This model shows that you must evolve through lower levels of behavior to higher levels in an orderly fashion. It is an evolutionary experience.

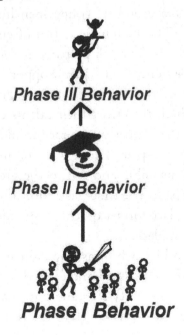

Phase III Behavior

Phase II Behavior

Phase I Behavior

Now I'd like to tell you a story in an effort to illustrate phase 3 behavior. It is a story about athletes with special needs. One of the organizations that support these athletes is the Special Olympics. So why was the Special Olympics organized? It began as a day camp in Maryland for children with intellectual disabilities, because Eunice Kennedy Shriver had a concern about disabled children with nowhere to play. Shriver promoted the concept of involvement in physical activity and competition opportunities for people with intellectual disabilities. Camp Shriver became an annual event, and the Kennedy Foundation campaigned to encourage individuals to stop using the word *retard* in everyday speech. It gave mentally-challenged people—a group of people whom we often perceive as being incapable of standing out in a crowd with their own natural skills and talents—a chance to stand out in a crowd. The Special Olympics organization has been an inspiration to many throughout its distinguished history.

Now here's a rather inspiring story that I believe was based on an actual event, but it came from the book *Chicken Soup for the Soul* written by Jack Canfield. I have added to the original story in hopes that it would be more effective in teaching you the desired lesson. Specifically, I have added the father and the coach characters to the story.

As the story goes, a group of young men lined up for the final race of the Olympics. The stadium was full of enthusiastic fans. The coaches were at the end of the track prepared to motivate their athletes. It was considered to be a once-in-a-lifetime opportunity for these young athletes to stand out in a crowd. The starting gun sounded, and the athletes took off with all the effort their talents could afford. It soon became obvious who the winner of the race would be as he pulled out yards ahead of the second-place runner. Then, unexpectedly, the last-place runner twisted his ankle and fell to the ground, screaming out from the excruciating pain. The first-place runner heard his screams and stopped. The second-place runner quickly responded and took over the desired position of first place.

The father of the athlete who was originally in first place threw his hat on the ground and said, "This handicapped stuff is very difficult—here my son had an opportunity to stand out in a crowd, and he blew the opportunity. Damn it!" The coach at the end of the lane stomped his foot on the ground and walked away in disgust. Soon all the athletes stopped in an attempt to figure out the cause of the screaming. Everyone witnessing the event watched as all the athletes stopped and walked back to the injured athlete. Eventually the original first-place runner reached out his hand to the injured athlete and lifted him up. The audience gasped as they watched the athletes put their arms around one another's shoulders and walk down the track, all crossing the line in first place. I often ask my leadership students, "Makes you wonder a little bit, doesn't it? Doesn't it make you wonder, just a little bit, who the truly handicapped ones are?"

Phase 3 behavior is willing to sacrifice its own glory to allow others to stand out in a crowd. In other words, phase 3 motives are pure. By pure motive, I mean the only reason for phase 3 action is to lift others up, not to draw attention to oneself. When phase 2 behavior performs acts that benefit society, it does so for its own self-glorification. Phase 3 behavior performs acts to benefit society; however, it does so strictly for the benefit of others, not for self-glorification. This is what makes phase 3 behavior unique.

There was a time when NBA Jazz tickets were given away anonymously in the Salt Lake Valley area. (The Jazz are an NBA basketball team.) I was a witness to one of these occasions when I met a young lady who worked for one of my clients. This young lady was the biggest Jazz fan I had ever met. Her cubical was totally decorated in Jazz memorabilia. On occasion I would stop and talk to her about the recent Jazz games. She loved to relive the biggest plays of the game. I once asked her if she had ever been to a Jazz game. She replied that she could never afford such a luxury. Later I found out that she was a single mother, and besides that, she didn't earn much money (she was just scraping by). As the years went by, I would stop and visit with her about the latest information on the Jazz's performance.

One day I was walking by her cubical and noticed that she had her head in her hands and was crying. I went in and asked her what was wrong. I asked her several times, and she wouldn't answer. Finally I decided that it must not be any of my business, so I apologized and was starting to leave when she called out my name. When I heard my name, I turned around, and an envelope hit me right in the chest. I caught the envelope and then opened it up and looked inside. I was shocked to find what appeared to be thousands of dollars' worth of Jazz tickets. Not only were there a lot of tickets, but they were in excellent locations. So I stopped and looked at them for a moment, and then I sat down and asked her if I could have one. (Just kidding—I didn't really ask her that.) I asked her where she got all the tickets. She said she had come to her office that morning, and they were sitting on her chair. I then asked her who had given her the tickets. She said there was no note or anything that would allow her to identify the Good Samaritan.

She desired to thank someone, so she called up the Jazz ticket office and told them she had found some tickets and desired to return them to the rightful owner. She read off the tracking number of one of the tickets. The lady on the other end of the phone line asked her to hold while she investigated. Eventually she came back and told my friend that she could not help her as the owner had paid cash for the tickets. The generous sly dog who purchased those tickets was untraceable! I don't know who gave those tickets away, but I assumed it was one of the vice presidents, as they were all paid well and never seemed to be shy about sharing their wealth with others on occasion. I don't know who bought those tickets for that lady, but I do know this: on that person's way to the ticket counter, emotions evaporated, and the only thing that allowed the person to follow through with the good deed was strength of character.

This story is a good example of phase 3 behavior in that someone sacrificed for someone else with no apparent desire to be recognized for the good deed. Phase 3 behavior demands sacrifice, and sacrifice demands character. Character is defined as the ability to follow through with a decision long after the emotion of making that decision is gone.

For example, imagine yourself being a child again, and everyone is always asking you, "What are you going to be when you grow up?" You notice that you get a pretty good response when you tell them you are going to be a surgeon someday. Enjoying the attention, you start telling everyone you are going to be a surgeon when you grow up. Eventually the thought of becoming a surgeon becomes an emotionally packed dream. Then you grow up and finally go to college and take your first difficult class. It is the first time you have ever had to sacrifice for the dream. When sacrifice meets emotion, emotions evaporate. Now, that's an important concept to remember: when sacrifice meets emotion, emotions evaporate, and the only thing that will determine whether you continue on with the dream is if you have enough character. Whether this young man will ever realize his dreams to be a surgeon will depend upon his ability to follow through with his decision long after the emotions of making that decision are gone. In other words, his dream will not be realized unless he has enough character.

I still remember the day the movie *Rocky* arrived at the local theaters. I went with all my neighborhood friends. When we got out of the theater, everyone was on an emotional high and wanted to be Rocky Balboa. Now, if you haven't seen *Rocky*, it's a rather emotionally action-packed film about an underdog fighter who goes out and fights for the championship. There were several *Rocky* movies, but if I remember correctly, in the first one he may not have won, but he came close to winning, and it really got people emotional about the sport of boxing, especially a group of young boys.

One of the things Rocky did when he was working out was that he'd drink raw eggs. So the next morning my friends and I got up and knocked down some raw eggs and took off running. We ran until we started hurting. Remember that when sacrifice meets emotions, emotions evaporate. Well, as soon as the sacrifice began, the emotions left, and we stopped running. We did not have the strength of character to become like Rocky. Life can be that way if we let it. Remember that phase 3 behavior demands sacrifice, and sacrifice demands character. If you are incapable of sacrifice, then you are not capable of performing phase 3 behavior—it's impossible. Sometimes phase 3 behavior even demands that you sacrifice your own popularity.

I love to read the books from Jack Welch. Jack Welch is a former CEO of General Electric, and in his book *Jack: Straight from the Gut* he told of an experience he had as a young man. It was the last game of the hockey season for Jack, and his team desperately wanted to end it on a positive note. As the story goes, the game went into overtime, and ultimately they lost. Jack was very upset and vented his frustration by throwing his hockey stick across the rink. He then skated out, picked up the stick, and went off to the locker room. As Jack tells it, he entered the locker room and saw his friends stripping off their pads when all of a sudden his Irish mother crashed through the locker room door and grabbed him by his jersey. Jack tells how the place fell silent.

Quoted directly from his book, he writes, "Every eye was glued on this middle-aged woman in a floral-patterned dress as she walked across the floor past the wooden benches where some of the guys were already changing. She went right for me, grabbing the top of my uniform. 'You punk!' she shouted in my face. 'If you don't know how to lose, you'll never know how to win. If you don't know this, you shouldn't be playing.'"

Obviously, this could have been a rather embarrassing moment for Jack, but we have all probably experienced similar situations in life. You know, it's a mom thing. I don't know exactly how Jack felt about this, but I know how I have felt in similar situations. I would have thought, *You are the meanest woman on the face of the earth. How dare you embarrass me in front of my friends like that?*

But as we mature, we realize that our mothers desired to lift us up to our true potential (that perhaps only they could see) and that they were willing to sacrifice their own popularity on our behalf. So remember that phase 3 behavior demands sacrifice, and sacrifice demands character, and sometimes we must sacrifice our own popularity to lift others up. This is especially true when we have a larger vision than the organization we're trying to lift up. In other words, in the organization's current state it is incapable of perceiving our vision of a better tomorrow. When this is the case, it is pretty standard that the group receiving this phase 3 behavior perceives it as phase 1 behavior.

Now, back to our beloved Jazz ticket story. It is worth repeating again: character is the ability to follow through with a decision long after the emotions of making that decision are gone. Remember that you cannot perform phase 3 behavior if you do not have the character demanded by the specific task.

I always give my students a homework assignment that I cannot grade. The homework assignment is to go out and do something good for someone else and never, ever let anyone know about the service provided or the sacrifice involved. This is the only way I know to prove that they are capable of phase 3 behavior or have evolved to the point that phase 3 behavior is a possibility.

The following story is one I like to share to illustrate the phase 3 behavior phenomena. There was a time in my life when I was fortunate enough to become a plant manager. On my first day on the job, I went around and introduced myself to all the employees. I met a young man whose name was Tom. I called him Tommy. I introduced myself, shook his hand, and asked him how everything was going. He told me that "things would be a hell of a lot better if those bastards on the other end of the line would pull their heads out." Tommy went on and on, and it felt very good to finally get away from him. Tommy was the most phase 1 person I had ever met in my life. I never really went around Tommy after that day, because it was just too depressing. I would always stay about fifty yards away, and if he looked at me, I would wave. That is pretty much how everyone treated Tommy. Don't get me wrong; Tommy was a hard worker. It was just his attitude that I had a difficult time stomaching.

I once asked one of the employees who had grown up in the same town as Tommy if he had known Tommy while they were growing up. He said, "Yes, I knew him all right. I used to feel sorry for him until he beat me up a few times." He then looked me right in the eye and said, "To be right honest with you, if Tommy died tomorrow, I wouldn't even shed a tear." In summary, no one liked to spend time with Tommy; he was just too much of a downer.

The manufacturing plant where the majority of this story took place had a problem. It was not just a plant problem; it was an industry problem. Whoever solved this problem would gain market share, increase profitability, and achieve job security for all the employees. This problem had been worked on for years before I ever arrived at the plant. At every production meeting for the last several years, the plant manager would ask for updates on a solution to this problem. Out of respect for this tradition, I would ask the same question, day in and day out. I was so accustomed to asking the question and getting the same answer that I stopped listening for the response from the production supervisor. Then one day, during the traditional production meeting, I asked the question, "How are we doing on the problem?"

The production supervisor quietly said, "Problem solved."

It didn't register, and I skipped to the next bullet point. Then the meaning of what he had just said struck me. I stopped, looked up, and said, "What did you say?"

He smiled back and said, "Problem solved!"

I threw my pen across the table and said, "You have got to be kidding me."

He then said, "No, it's true."

Then, while rubbing my brow, I looked up and said, "Who solved the problem?"

The supervisor quickly answered, "Tommy solved the problem."

I gasped and then quietly laughed and said, "You have got to be kidding me."

I thought in my mind, *What is this? Is it April Fool's Day or something?* Then I looked over at the production supervisor with a look that said, *We shouldn't be joking around about this.*

He then took his hat off, ran his fingers through his hair, and said, "No, really, John. Tommy solved the problem."

I put my elbows up on the table, rested my chin in my hands, looked him straight in the eye, and said, "Tommy solved it? Maybe I misread the kid."

The supervisor responded, "Maybe." The supervisor explained the solution to the problem, and all of a sudden it made so much sense. I thought to myself, *Why didn't I think of that?*

After the meeting, I reluctantly swallowed my pride and went out to Tommy's workstation and told him, "Hey, Tommy. I heard you solved the problem. Is that true?"

He responded harshly, "Who told you that?"

I swallowed my pride and said, "That's what your supervisor told me." Tommy then stood up a little taller, and with his typical, angry-sounding voice, he said, "Yeah, so what's it to ya?"

I swallowed my pride again, for the second time now, and said, "Thank you for all that you have done for this company. You have created job security for everyone."

He then quickly looked at the ground and turned away from me and said, "Sounds like a bunch of BS to me."

I then swallowed my pride again, now for the third time, and said, talking to his back, "I am going to talk to the VP and see if I can't come up with a reward for you."

Tommy didn't respond, and I took a drive to go break the good news to the VP. Ultimately, the VP was very excited about the news and agreed to give Tommy five thousand dollars for his successful efforts. However, he told me I was not allowed to present the check to Tommy until the company Christmas party.

Before we go any further, I should probably give you some background on Tommy. You see, Tommy was born to a drug-addicted, prostitute mother. He never knew his father. Growing up, he lived in a camp trailer with his mother and younger brother. They lived right off the bottom edge of a huge lake, and in the winter when the winds would come off the lake, it would get extremely cold. The poorer people in town would heat their trailers with kerosene lanterns or heaters. One evening Tommy's mother was out doing her thing, and Tommy and his younger brother were in the camp trailer playing with a ball. When the younger brother threw Tommy the ball, it accidently hit the kerosene heater. The heater fell from the shelf and broke open when it hit the floor. The floor was covered with burning kerosene. Tommy's brother escaped out the front door without injury, but Tommy was not so lucky. He had to run through the slick, burning kerosene. In doing so, he slipped and fell, burying the left side of his face in the burning kerosene. He got up and ran around the trailer screaming with half of his face ablaze. He eventually jumped in a snow bank and put out the fire. By the time he jumped into the snow bank, the damage had already been done. Half of Tommy's face was melted. It was so damaged that he would never fully recover. The left side of his face looked like melted plastic.

From time to time, we would provide plant tours for customers, suppliers, and others. I would always warn them about Tommy's face in hopes that they would not gasp and embarrass themselves. I told the visitors that if they did gasp, not to worry. It seemed that Tommy had learned how to deal with it over time, but despite the warning, they would gasp anyway. Tommy didn't seem to notice. Imagine how Tommy must have felt going to grade school! Eventually, he found out how he could stand out in a crowd. He could be ornery and nasty and

23

beat people up if they as much as looked at him sideways, and he became rather good at beating people up.

You know, most people have parents or other significant people who can champion them through life. Tommy did not have that luxury. He had to become tough; he also had to learn how to effectively use phase I methodologies to give himself a feeling of value. Remember the two assumptions of the model. The first one was the mother of all motivators is survival. And number two was if you can't stand out in a crowd, you will die. Tommy was just trying to survive the only way he knew how.

Anyway, back to the story. Tommy had supposedly solved the problem. In reality, I never really believed he had solved the problem. I felt the only person in that plant who had the skills and talents necessary to solve that problem was Tommy's supervisor. This supervisor was in my office once, and I told him that I didn't think Tommy had solved that problem. I told the supervisor that I thought he was the one who had solved the problem. After I communicated this to him, he got mad; he went ballistic. He told me that if I wanted to believe my own lie, then go ahead, but it was just that—a lie. He then stomped out of my office. Now I have to tell you, I'm not really sharp all the time, but I did realize that was a subject I didn't want to visit again. I never brought up the topic to Tommy's supervisor again.

Time went by, and we eventually had a company Christmas party. We rented the local high school auditorium, and everyone showed up for the anticipated annual event. I went to the party, stood up on the stage, and made some generic announcements, and then I told them we had someone to honor. I told them there was a young man who had gone the extra mile and solved an important problem for the company. I told them that this young man had brought job security to everyone in that auditorium, and we should be appreciative of what he had done. Then I told them it was Tommy—that Tommy had solved the problem that brought job security to everyone in the auditorium. I called Tommy up to the stand and ushered him up to the podium next to me. I paused a minute and told the audience, "This is the young man who made the difference." I wasn't really expecting what happened next. The audience stood up and gave Tommy a standing ovation.

I never told anyone, but I saw tears well up in the corner of Tommy's eyes as he stared at the floor and walked from the stage. Looking back, I realize that was probably the first time Tommy had ever stood out in a crowd based on his perceived skills and talents. Tommy got a lot of pats on the back that night and eventually seemed to rise to the occasion.

One morning I had to go in especially early to the plant; it was approximately four o'clock in the morning. As I passed by Tommy's supervisor's office, I noticed that his light was on. Out of curiosity, I peeked through the window on the door. I was shocked at what I saw; the supervisor was in his office with his hat off, lecturing Tommy on problem-solving methodologies. Now I knew for sure who had actually solved that problem. Past experience suggested that I dare not mention it to anyone, which I didn't until I wrote this book.

Being a little humbled from past experience, I decided to give Tommy another chance. I was pleasantly surprised when I went up and asked him how he was doing, and all he wanted to talk about were problems he was working on. Unbelievable! Tommy had actually learned how to stand out in a crowd based on his new skills and talents, and he loved it. He was, no kidding, a different person. Tommy had evolved to phase 2 behavior right before my eyes.

I learned a couple of lessons from this experience. First, don't look at phase I behavior as bad or evil; instead, look at it as people just trying to survive the only way they know how. The second lesson I was taught was the power of phase 3 behavior. I witnessed phase 3 behavior from that supervisor, who changed a person right before my very eyes. I learned that changing culture is ultimately about changing people.

In summary, phase 3 behavior is the only form of behavior capable of changing culture in a positive way. Phase 3 behavior, then, is the essence of leadership. Remember that leadership in the world of transformation means the ability to change culture, and the ability to change culture is the ability to change people. Phase I behavior is not capable of changing culture for the good, neither is phase 2, at least to any significant extent. So if we are to become capable of changing culture (which is leadership), we must learn to master the art of phase 3 behavior.

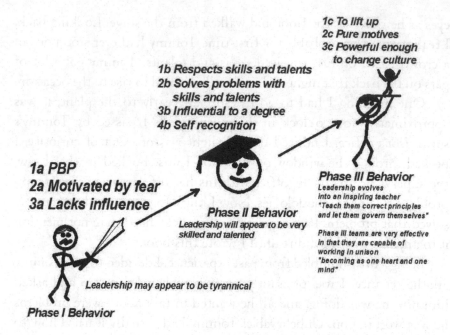

1c To lift up
2c Pure motives
3c Powerful enough
to change culture

1b Respects skills and talents
2b Solves problems with
skills and talents
3b Influential to a degree
4b Self recognition

1a PBP
2a Motivated by fear
3a Lacks influence

Phase III Behavior
Leadership evolves
into an inspiring teacher
"Teach them correct principles
and let them govern themselves"

Phase II Behavior
Leadership will appear to be very
skilled and talented

Phase III teams are very effective
in that they are capable of
working in unison
"becoming as one heart and one
mind"

Leadership may appear to be tyrannical

Phase I Behavior

Now let's update our model and review it again. Remember that phase I behavior tends to solve problems with personify, blame, and punish methodologies. Also remember that personify, blame, and punish has the natural by-product of fear. In addition, phase I behavior is motivated by fear and lacks influence. Often it is difficult to tell on the leadership side when you first go into a phase I organization whether the leader is exercising phase I behavior. Does the leadership have higher motives but realize that the organization has to be managed with fear because its members respect nothing else? After a short time, however, you can tell which kind of leader you have, because a phase 3 leader will use fear to get the organization under control and then evolve the organization. So if you see an individual come in using fear as the motivator and then evolve the organization into higher levels of behavior, such as phase 2, then that person is a good leader.

Bad leaders motivate the organization by fear just because they are phase I individuals and haven't evolved yet. An indication of this is that they can never sustain a performance rating much over 95 percent. If that's the case, they will never evolve their organizations beyond the point where they just want control and are willing to exercise fear in the long term to keep that control. Remember—you never become greater than that which motivates you.

Now, for phase 2 behavior, remember that it is about respect for skills and talents, so if you're going to lead a phase 2 organization, the workers have to respect you if they're going to let you lead them. Therefore, you have to show them that you have greater skills and talents than they have. If the workers perceive they have better skills and talents than you do, they will stop respecting you, and you will not be able to lead the organization, because they will most likely try to undermine you. Remember that phase 2 individuals solve problems with their skills and talents. Also, remember that phase 2 is influential to a degree and likes self-recognition. Phase 2 individuals will do a lot of things to make themselves look good in the end, because self-glorification is their motive.

Now, with phase 3 behavior, remember that key words are "to lift up"—lifting others up with a pure motive of lifting them up, making people feel better about what they can accomplish, and lifting them up just for them, not for you. You do not try to draw attention to yourself for your good deeds. Phase 3 behavior is powerful enough to change culture. In other words, it's powerful enough to change people. And phase 3 behavior, if you'll recall, demands sacrifice, and sacrifice demands character. So what does a leader do in a phase 3 organization? Well, if you're talented enough to get an organization up to phase 3 behavior, leadership becomes rather easy for most people. You see, the leader becomes the teacher. That's right. To lead a phase 3 organization, you must evolve into a teacher. In other words, you teach people correct principles and then let them govern themselves. Phase 3 behavior will never embarrass you, which means it will never fail you.

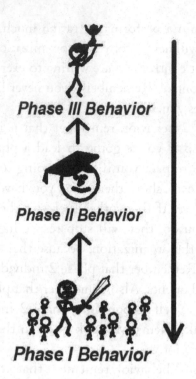

Phase III Behavior

Phase II Behavior

Phase I Behavior

Thus far I have taught that once you evolve upward from phase 1 to phase 2 and ultimately phase 3 behavior, you stay at the higher levels of behavior. This is not true. Once you achieve higher levels of behavior, you can still slide down to lower levels of behavior. If you ultimately evolve to be capable of phase 3 behavior, there are forces that can cause you to act out in lower levels of behavior. What are these forces? Well, remember that phase 3 behavior demands sacrifice, and sacrifice demands character. The problem source is that no one has infinite character, so you can only stay in phase 3 behavior according to the amount of character you have achieved. If the sacrifice demands more character than you currently have, then you will slide down to lower levels of behavior.

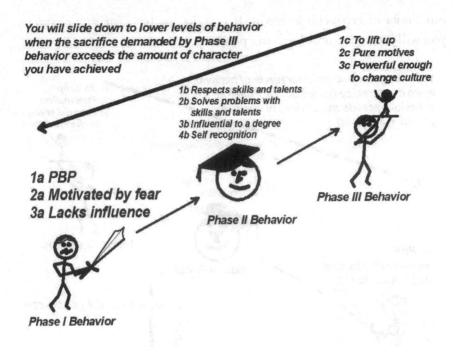

You will slide down to lower levels of behavior when the sacrifice demanded by Phase III behavior exceeds the amount of character you have achieved

1c To lift up
2c Pure motives
3c Powerful enough to change culture

1b Respects skills and talents
2b Solves problems with skills and talents
3b Influential to a degree
4b Self recognition

1a PBP
2a Motivated by fear
3a Lacks influence

Phase III Behavior

Phase II Behavior

Phase I Behavior

Let's add another element to the model. Remember that you will slide down to lower levels of behavior when the sacrifice demanded by phase 3 behavior exceeds the amount of character you have achieved in life. So in your phase 3 behavior, you start experiencing stress. By stress I mean that you're asked to sacrifice more than you're capable of sacrificing. At this point, you go into phase 2 where you may think or say something like, "Okay, get out of the room. I'll solve this problem myself." If the pressure keeps building, the sacrifice demands more and more, and you don't have enough character to sustain it, then you can fall into phase I behavior, where you start acting out personify, blame, and punish. In other words, the more character you have, the more influential you are capable of becoming because you will be able to sustain higher levels of human behavior under higher levels of stress. Keep in mind what character is: the ability to follow through with a decision long after the emotions of making that decision are gone.

Concerning human behavior, infinite character equals infinite influence. The problem is that none of us has infinite character; thus, we will not have infinite influence. However, we can raise our character and increase our influence over time. We often refer to the act of reaching our limits of character as stress. If you do not have infinite character, you will have a natural breaking point.

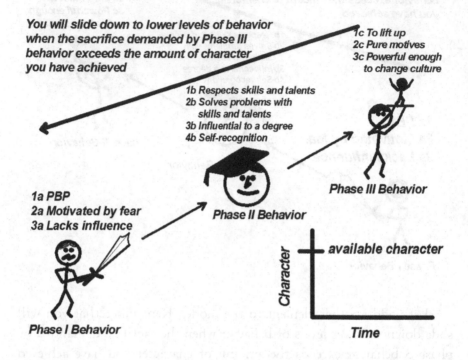

You will slide down to lower levels of behavior when the sacrifice demanded by Phase III behavior exceeds the amount of character you have achieved

1c To lift up
2c Pure motives
3c Powerful enough
*   to change culture*

1b Respects skills and talents
2b Solves problems with
*   skills and talents*
3b Influential to a degree
4b Self-recognition

1a PBP
2a Motivated by fear
3a Lacks influence

Phase III Behavior

Phase II Behavior

available character

Character

Time

Phase I Behavior

Notice that down in the right-hand corner of the figure above I have added a little chart that shows the available character. You can maintain the higher level of behavior as long as your available character is above the character that is needed to perform the task. But as the task increases and more sacrifice is demanded of you, it works its way up that axis until eventually the character needed is above the character available. That is the point where you'll start sliding down into lower levels of behavior. I refer to it as the breaking point. The good news in all this is that through life's experiences, we can achieve or we can grow our character.

When I was just a young boy, I had a problem. Like most little boys, I desired to be courageous. The problem was that even though I desired the attribute of courage, I was just a big chicken, and everyone knew it. One day I sat down and talked to my grandfather, to whom I was very close, and I told him I had a problem. He sat down and asked me to describe my problem to him. I quietly told my grandfather that I desired to be courageous.

He looked at me for a moment in shock and then said, "You do have a problem." Again, everyone knew I was a chicken.

I looked at my wonderful grandfather and said, "What do I need to do to become courageous?"

My grandfather then got a serious look on his face and started rubbing his chin. This was a sign that he was thinking hard, so I just sat there and watched him do all the work. Then, to my great relief, I saw the countenance of his face light up, and I knew he had the answer for me. With excitement, I told him, "Give me the answer, Grandfather; please give me the answer."

He said, "The answer is in the movie you watched last night." I asked him, "What movie was that?"

He reminded me that I had watched *The Wizard of Oz* and pointed out that one of the characters in the movie had the same problem I had just described. I thought back for a moment and then remembered that it was the lion. The lion wanted to be courageous, but he was a natural-born chicken just like I was. My grandfather encouraged me to come up with my own answer. He helped me by asking, "What did the lion do to get courage?"

I thought for a moment and then responded, "He went to Oz. The lion went to Oz, and Oz gave him courage. I remember now!"

My grandfather slapped his forehead and said, "Good grief, kid. You missed the whole meaning of the movie."

So I responded back at him, saying, "Then tell me the meaning of the movie."

After looking around the room and making sure my mother wasn't listening, he bent down by my ear and whispered, "The lion gained courage from his voyage to Oz, not from Oz; he overcame his fears by facing his fears." Then he paused for a moment and added, "You need to do everything that scares you over and over again until it doesn't scare you anymore. That was the point of the story. That's how the lion obtained the attribute of courage—by going against his fears, even though it was very uncomfortable for him."

So I did as my grandfather said. I made a mental note of all my fears and went out and began to face them. I ended up with a lot of scrapes and bruises, and slowly but surely, I started developing within myself the attribute of courage.

By the time I went to college, I had overcome many of my fears. Among my favorite hobbies was riding motocross bikes across the deserts of Idaho and racing stock cars on Saturday nights. By the time I went to college, I had won two series championships and one track championship at the local dirt track. I had overcome a lot of fears. With all that said, I still had one phobia that I needed to overcome, and that was my fear of heights. So while in college I picked up the sport of skydiving. To be honest with you, it was so scary to me that I can't even remember my first four jumps.

On my first jump, which was in Antioch, California, there was a camera attached to the aircraft wing, so it took a picture of me falling from the plane that very first time. And I can tell you this—I looked like a scared cat, and I felt like I looked. The scariest jump I remember was approximately my tenth jump. It had me so concerned that as I was walking across the campus to get to my next class, I would remember that I was scheduled to jump on the weekend and my palms would start sweating—and my palms don't usually sweat. It was a sobering week as I considered it may be my last week.

On Saturday morning, the morning of jump day—also remembered by me, in my mind anyway, as death day—I got up and cleaned my room. I remember thinking I may not be coming back, and I wanted to let my mom know she had taught me something. Then I got in my car and picked up my friend, who was also scheduled for his tenth jump. I could tell he was scared also, as nothing was said on our way to the airport. As we rode in the car, I started thinking strategically and reasoned that if I could get to the airplane first, then I would be the last one to get out of the plane; that would give me a few more breaths.

As we arrived at the airport, I quickly implemented the strategy and was the first to put on my parachute and get in the airplane. If I recall correctly, the plane was just a small Cessna Skyhawk 172, so there was not a lot of room; however, there was enough room for the pilot, the jumpmaster, and two jumpers. I was sitting on the floor with my knees up against my chest facing the back of the plane as the airplane began its climb to jump altitude, which was approximately six thousand feet above the ground.

I was attempting to enjoy what I perceived as the last moments of my life when I heard the door being pulled up on the old Cessna aircraft. This was always a violent experience, as the open door allows approximately one-hundred-mile-per-hour winds to enter the aircraft. Out of curiosity, I looked around at the front of the plane and noticed that the jumpmaster was hanging out the side of the plane, and I thought to myself, *This guy is nuts!* However, I was impressed at how he came in and out of the plane with no apparent fear; I hoped to have that level of courage someday. I also knew this was not going to be that day, as I was so scared that I was shaking.

The reason the jumpmaster was hanging out of the plane was that he was looking for the target. They actually put a target on the drop zone, and yes, it looked like a bull's-eye—which was kind of strange— but that was what he was doing. I personally never felt comfortable with the bull's-eye thing. I am not sure why; it just always made me feel uncomfortable. After getting over the target, the jumpmaster tapped my friend on the shoulder and told him it was time to get out. For beginners like me, getting out of the plane was not that easy. You had to first go from a sitting position to putting one foot out of the plane onto the landing gear. This is rather difficult with a one-hundred-mile-per-hour wind, especially with seeing the ground some six thousand feet below your foot, which does not help matters any.

The jumpmaster tapped my friend on the shoulder and told him it was time to get out, so my friend got his right foot on the landing gear. Then he had to twist his body out of the plane and quickly grab the diagonal structural strut with his left hand. Next he had to extend his right hand up farther on the strut. All of this had to be done in some high-wind velocities, and, yes, I have seen students slip, fall, and scream, understandably, as it is not a short fall.

Anyway, back to the story. My friend was now out of the plane and, as instructed, he had two hands on the strut and one foot on the locked landing gear. Sometimes they will joke around and not lock the wheel, and when someone steps on it, well, it's good-bye and adios. I always found that pretty funny—unless, of course, they did it to me; then I was fit to be tied. By this time, my friend's other foot, his right foot, was now dangling in the wind. I had moved into jump position, so the jumpmaster was leaning over me as he prepared to give instructions to my friend. I was now just a couple of feet from my friend, who was about to fall out of the airplane—at least that was my assumption.

While all this was happening I had not mustered up the courage to look outside, so I was just looking at the jumpmaster. After directing the plane directly over the drop zone target, the jumpmaster yelled out, "Ready, set, go!" My friend did not respond. As I glanced out, I noticed that his left foot had slipped off the landing gear, but he still had a hellish grip on the strut. I could not believe my eyes when I saw him just swinging back and forth on the wing. I was thinking, *How can you do this to me? These people are nutcases.*

Finally, the jumpmaster went through his countdown again, only louder this time. He said, "Ready, set, go!" I looked out of the plane again, and yes, my friend was still hanging out there. He was in his own world; he would not even look at the jumpmaster. I was now completely covered in sweat. This was worse than I had expected! I would prefer a quick death rather than dragging it out into infamy.

Anyway, the jumpmaster tried a few more times to get my friend to jump but with no response. I said, "Bye-bye, mental function." I was now watching the jumpmaster and wondering what he was going to do next. He looked over at the pilot and smiled and winked, and I thought, *You pervert. Here my friend is hanging out there on the wing, and you are enjoying yourself at his expense.* The next thing I remember is the plane going into a rather aggressive dive, and I was thinking, *What are you doing? Don't tell me you are going to try to land the plane with my friend out there.* The next thing I knew, we were pulling out of the dive, and I was being pushed into the floor of the plane by some respectable g-forces. At this point in time, I started becoming concerned about my friend again. I noticed that he was putting up a valiant fight as his knuckles were nearly transparent. As I saw it, it was now my friend against the pilot, and I must admit I was proud of the fight my friend was putting out. If I had not been so scared I would have been cheering for him out loud.

I then looked over at the jumpmaster and saw him look at the pilot in a way that said, *This guy is pretty good. Okay, not pretty good—this guy is amazing.*

Then I felt the response as the g-forces pressed me into the floor of the plane so hard I could no longer sit up straight. Lying on the floor, I now looked out at my friend, and what I saw was not pretty. He was still hanging there, but you could tell it was only a matter of time before the situation would resolve itself. It appeared to me that he was having convulsions out on the end of that wing while he was searching for the all-natural fetal position. Eventually the g-forces got the best of him, and away he went—good-bye, friend. I watched him as he faded away into the blue skies; as he fell away, he was reaching for the plane, and his pleading eyes were directly attached to mine and were clearly asking for help. I wish I could tell you I wanted to jump out and help him, but that would be a fallacy. I was more in the mood of saying, "You poor soul." Okay, okay, I said I wanted to be courageous. I was not yet courageous. These things take time—be patient.

Moving on with the story—the jumpmaster now looked into my mentally fatigued face and uttered the horrifying words, "John, it's your turn." He followed it up by patting me on the back and saying, "You can do this—just focus."

Just focus on what? I thought. *The ground six thousand feet below me? That is really smart—why don't I do that?!* Okay, I tend to get sarcastic when I think I'm about to die—sue me. Maybe he meant to focus on the warmth running down my leg? In the end, I am proud to tell you that I did as my jumpmaster told me and dug into my guts and got out on that wing. Before I left the plane, I noticed something that I had not noticed before. The strut was covered with a reddish transparent plastic cover, and it had scratch marks all over it. I even thought I saw a piece of fingernail—no kidding.

Now, finally, I want you to know that I did jump out of that plane. In fact, I jumped out of planes more than a hundred times after that, until I no longer feared the experience. But the point of the story is this: when you slide down the slope from higher levels of behavior to lower levels of behavior, remember to leave scratch marks.

I have been trying to live this phase 3 model most of my life, and even though I have a full understanding of the model, when I feel myself slipping again, even though I know what is happening, I cannot stop it, as I have reached the capability of my character and I helplessly fall to lower levels of behavior. But, I have also learned that if I leave scratch marks all the way down the curve and then aggressively claw my way back up, then my efforts are rewarded with an increase in character, which gives me the potential to be more influential in future situations.

I must admit the irony of the model is that you must fail to succeed. I know of no other way to gain additional character except by failing.

If you don't fail and fall down the curve, then you cannot put forth the effort to climb back up the curve. Fighting the fall and climbing back up the curve is what builds character.

I guess this is what makes Jack Welch's mom a genius when she said something to the effect of "you must learn how to lose before you can learn to win." If you're afraid to lose, then you will probably never leave the perceived comfort of phase 1 behavior, because you will be concerned about what happens if you fail. Remember that you can never become greater than that which motivates you, and if fear is your motivation of choice, then you will never climb out of the misery of phase 1 behavior.

So if you ever do evolve and find yourself capable of phase 3 behavior, but you build a life that never challenges your limited character and never allows you to fall down the curve, then you will no longer grow your ability to influence others—what a shame! Don't be afraid to fail. Failure is ultimately what allows growth to be realized. Always remember that a weakness is nothing more than a potential strength. If you go against a weakness long enough, it will eventually become your strength. In other words, the act of fighting to overcome your weaknesses creates strength, until someday you will have enough strength to overcome the weaknesses, and thus the weaknesses become strengths. It's quite simple really. Though a weakness *is* a potential strength, beware that phase 1 behavior does not see weaknesses that way. Phase 1 and some elements of phase 2 behaviors suggest that it is a flaw that should condemn you and because of your weaknesses you can never become great. To that I say ignore the critics and deal with the truth, and the truth is that without weaknesses, you would be incapable of creating strength. Weaknesses have the potential of being your greatest blessing in life, but not until you see them as potential strengths.

Remember that phase 1 behavior will belittle other people's weaknesses and hide its own. Thus, phase 1 behavior does not allow personal or organizational growth. Phase 1 behavior is incapable of transformation. Phase 3 behavior, on the other hand, sees weaknesses as potential strengths. Phase 3 behavior does not hide weaknesses but puts them out in the open and works them over in an intelligent manner. Phase 3 behavior will not make fun of people or organizations for weaknesses. It makes no sense to phase 3 behavior to belittle potential strength. Where is the logic in that?

When you bottom out on phase 1, the phase 1 environment will say, "I see you have bottomed out in phase 1. You are worthless and can never climb the curve of human behavior again." I have always argued that God gave man a middle finger for a reason. Nothing is more destructive to the human soul than to believe, incorrectly so, that because of your weakness you can't get better. In reality, it is just the opposite. You can become stronger because of your weaknesses. In my opinion, we shouldn't call them weaknesses at all, because that has a negative context. Instead, we should call them potential strengths. I honestly feel that my potential strengths are gifts from whoever created me. My greatest gift back will be to rise above any weaknesses and bring them back as strengths, which is my goal in life. If He didn't want us to have weaknesses, He would have created us accordingly. So in short, ignore the critics, get to work, and climb the curve. The only reason critics have power over you is because you care what they think. Rise above it all.

While criticism can be a good thing, people can only handle it if it is constructive, in the right doses, and, perhaps, the right timing. So if you find yourself being criticized and you're not ready for it, just become indifferent to it. Your critics will learn rather quickly that they have no power over you and will leave you alone, because they realize that you won't give them what they want—satisfaction. The only reason negative critics have power over you is because you let them. Rise above it all.

I can still fondly remember the day I realized I had gained the attribute of courage, which resulted from overcoming my weaknesses—I mean, my potential strengths. It took a lot of work getting there, and I came within fractions of a second of dying on multiple occasions, but for me, it was worth it.

The evening I remember overcoming my fear was when I was jumping in Northern California. I was standing on the edge of a Beechcraft ready to leap into another skydiving experience from twelve thousand feet. I just stood there for a moment and looked at the beauty of the California sunset. Then, without fear of death or anything else, I sailed into the beautiful bronze sky. I never remember experiencing such freedom as I did that day, as I had freed myself from the most enslaving and crippling practice of all—fear. Fear is ultimately nothing more than a lack of hope, and in the end, I discovered that I didn't really need to jump out of planes to gain courage. I could have just taught myself to appreciate the past; it gives me the same rush and feeling of a freed soul.

If you really desire to tick me off, try motivating me with fear. I consider that the biggest insult anyone could give me. The gall to thi k I would choose such a poor motivator is truly insulting to me, as it should be to you. I have worked too hard to be motivated by such a stupid motive. Rise above it all!

In the world of skydiving, the term *blue skies* is used. The term *blue skies* means "have a great day," or perhaps a great jump, or, in certain special situations, "have a great life by living a great life." On that day, the term *blue skies* seemed to have more meaning to me. I had finally risen above it all.

Phase 3 behavior, by its very nature, is free of fear. Once you taste phase 3 behavior, you will never want to go back to lower levels of behavior, and you will do whatever you can to return to its peaceful and productive environment. Why? Because it feels better—again, pretty simple. For the most part, everything around us is simple.

Another thing to remember is that phase 1 behavior will always make fun of phase 3 behavior. Phase 1 behavior fantasizes about destroying phase 3 behavior. The bigger and more important someone appears to be, the more enjoyable it is to see that person fall. The conflict between phase 1 and phase 3 behavior is a natural one but also very unique because phase 3 behavior is willing to help those who, at times, desire to destroy them.

Now I would like to review some very important thoughts. Remember that if you are afraid to fail, you may not fail, but if you do not fail, you cannot succeed, for at some level success demands failure. Redundant failure ultimately allows success to be realized. By not giving up on overcoming weaknesses, you will forge the weaknesses into strengths. Effort is your hammer; weakness is your raw material. Get to work—rise above it all. Ultimately, phase 3 behavior is about rising above it all. So rise above it all. Don't be afraid.

I will end this chapter with some thoughts concerning leadership and the importance that leadership plays in lifting up organizations (organizational transformation). A leader can never raise an organization above his predominant level of personal behavior. A phase 1 behavior leader is incapable of raising an organization up to phase 2 behavior, but a phase 2 leader is capable of raising an organization up to phase 2 behavior. Phase 3 organizations are not easy to find. In all the organizations I have toured throughout the world, I have found a few that I would say are phase 3 organizations or companies.

One such company I did find is a division of US Synthetic, a company that manufactures synthetic diamonds in Orem, Utah. The top value of their organization is to change lives. When I toured this plant, I knew I had found something special, so I tried to find out more about their leader. Through my investigation, I found the company's CEO had recently retired. It didn't surprise me, nor should it surprise you, what I discovered. I asked where he retired to and was told that he had moved to Africa and was helping to build schoolhouses for the children. There are as many phase 3 organizations as there are phase 3 leaders. I rest my case.

One phenomenon that is fairly common throughout history is when a phase 2 leader decides to create a utopia—utopia being defined as a society where everyone exhibits phase 3 behavior. Bearing in mind that phase 2 behavior tends to seek self-glorification. The objective of creating a utopia is so that the leader can get recognition for being great. I refer to this as fantasy statue building. The leader will attempt to force phase 3 behavior upon the people. This is foolishness, for phase 3 behavior cannot be forced; it can only be nurtured. Ultimately, these utopias will fail unless there is an influential phase 3 leader. Because phase 3 behavior cannot be forced, attempting to force phase 3 behavior is a moral perversion that will ultimately create destructive behavior. One reason for this phenomenon is that leaders must lead by example to lead organizations to higher levels of human behavior; leadership is the constraint of social evolution.

Remember you cannot raise up another unless you are standing on higher ground.

Chapter Four

Rules of Phase 3 Behavior

One rule of transformation is that you will not change the organization's personality or culture by accident. If you are going to change culture, you had better understand and implement the principles of influence. Culture is very difficult to change, and it is the most difficult of all the elements of organizational transformation.

Phase 3 behavior is the only form of human behavior that truly allows for a more fulfilling and productive life.

One of the objectives of this lesson is to teach the principles of influence, often referred to as the principles of a more fulfilling and productive life. My experience has dictated that there are certain rules that a person must follow to have the influence necessary to transform to what I call a level of greatness. Transforming to higher levels of fulfillment demands passion and belief that the seemingly impossible is possible and obtainable. Transformation to greatness demands that people exercise passionate appreciation for their own legacies.

The objective of this chapter is to tell you about the rules of fulfillment (rules of greatness) in hopes that you will exercise them in your life and, as a result, find your true potential and the ultimate potential of organizations that you serve. There are fourteen rules of greatness.

Rule I

You will never become great if you never desire to be great. Greatness

48

is defined as reaching one's ultimate potential or the potential of that organization. We are currently in the dark ages of our human potential.

Desire. What creates desire? What is desire? There is an evolution of human thought. The thought starts as a hypothesis. If the hypothesis proves to have predictable abilities, it may evolve into a theory. If the theory is never found to be incorrect in its predictive abilities, then it becomes a law. Laws will ultimately breed objectivity, and this objectivity will ultimately serve human needs. Laws have the potential to improve the human condition.

One such law is referred to as the law of entropy. Entropy is a measure of disorder. The law of entropy states that a system will become more and more disorganized over time unless energy is added to the system. Scientists have never found an exception to this law. That's why it is referred to as a law. For example, if you never tidy your living quarters, they will tend to become more and more disorganized over time. No one in all of history has witnessed his living quarters becoming cleaner and more organized while doing nothing. People do not necessarily appreciate the law of entropy. It means that we have to perform work if we're to maintain things or to make them better. Laws are generally simple statements and difficult to argue with. So becoming more and more disorganized is only natural. Desire will ultimately reveal itself by creating a more orderly environment.

Desire is not a natural state. This is why desire ultimately has to be a conscious choice; it will not happen by accident. The by-product of desire is sacrifice. If someone says he has a desire, then you should be able to witness that person performing sacrifice. If a person says he has desire but is unwilling to sacrifice, then the conscious decision of desire has not yet been made. Desire is the fuel that drives transformation.

Somehow human beings are more capable of conscious desire than other creatures, and as a result, we are more capable of improving our environment. Why some desire to rise above nature and make things better and others are content to let things degrade into natural destruction is a question that has been asked and unanswered throughout the ages. Ultimately, desire is the decision to rise above it all, whatever the sacrifice may be. The cycle of tyranny to anarchy and back to tyranny again is a natural state of affairs.

Freedom is not a natural state of being. Freedom from tyranny is only realized when people desire to be free. As soon as people lose their desire to be free, then nature will take over and freedom will be lost. Ultimately, freedom demands desire, and desire demands sacrifice. The founding fathers of the United States desired freedom. They made a choice to rise above the natural cycle of tyranny to anarchy, no matter what the cost.

One such individual was one of wealthiest people in the colonies. He chose to make a difference in the cause of freedom, whatever the sacrifice was. This individual volunteered his time and energy in the cause of freedom. He did not accept a salary; he only accepted expenses after his efforts proved successful. When his inexperienced troops seemed fearful on the eve of battle, he stepped up to the challenge and rode his horse back and forth in the front of the line. The adversarial army opened fire on him with both cannons and muskets; his men were inspired by his courage as he led them into the sacrifice for freedom that we call war.

Miraculously, this person's body was never pierced by the enemy's bullets. He sacrificed on the field of battle for six long, discouraging years. Toward the end of the war, he went home for the first time. During this short visit home, his only son practically demanded that his father let him become part of this war for freedom. Ultimately, his father gave in and allowed the son to join the war effort. After the war was won and everyone was celebrating the seemingly impossible victory, this person went home, and alongside his wife, the mother of his child, he mourned the death of his only son, who had died in the fight for freedom.

Oh, I forgot to tell you that this person also led an army made up of men who were seldom paid, or properly fed, for that matter. There was a point in time when it got so bad that his valued military leaders decided to attack the Congress, which was incapable of living up to the contract it had signed with the soldiers concerning pay. It seemed that the unnatural act of freedom would have to wait for another day. This individual knew that he must act if the cause of freedom was to be realized.

He entered into the hall where everyone met before moving on to take over the Continental Congress. He tried to reason with them, but he could tell by their body language that they refused to be softened. Out of desperation, he thought about what he could do to save the situation.

From his perspective, the results of all their sacrifices and the unnatural act of freedom were about to be lost.

After talking at length with these military leaders, it appeared to him that nothing he said was going to change their minds. He then remembered a letter that he had tucked away in his coat; he felt that this letter may soften the men. He quickly pulled the note out of his coat and tried to read it, but he could not, as his eyes were worn with age. He quickly dug for his spectacles as the men watched; this shocked the soldiers, because they had never seen him use spectacles before. They considered him to be somewhat immortal and must have thought to themselves, *Is this not the same man who rode into battle before us and could not be hit by the bullets of men? Why would such a man need spectacles?* In that silent moment, they realized he was human like they were.

As the man began to put on his spectacles, he said something like this: "I'm sorry. I fear that I have worn myself out in service to my country."

All the military leadership knew that this man had volunteered his time and energy and that he would give up everything he owned to serve this ideal of freedom. The fact that he had sacrificed more than they had turned out to be very influential.

I am not certain what that letter said. I do believe it was from a congressman or a senator, but in the end, it doesn't really matter, because when they heard the words "I have worn myself out in service to my country," all the men began to cry. They all knew that no one had sacrificed more than he. The thoughts of destroying the fragile new country and falling back into the natural cycle of the human condition—that of tyranny, anarchy, and back to tyranny—would have to wait, for desire had been restored. The fall to nature would have to wait for yet another day.

I have had people argue with me that this person had flaws of his own and therefore does not deserve the accolades that I so freely give him. I studied deeper and found it to be true—this person was very much human. But instead of discouraging me, it only inspired me more. What I found is that imperfect people can do perfect things. This discovery was very liberating for me. Perhaps even I could make a difference for the good! Remember that you do not have to be perfect to create perfection and do perfect things. You can be successful at something bigger than yourself.

For all that is spoken concerning perfection, I must confess that I have never met a perfect person. That is correct—not even one. Even though I have sat through many meetings demanding that people be perfect, I have never witnessed the goal of perfection being obtained and/or sustained. From this perspective, I must say that perfection is overrated, and the journey to perfection is underrated. This man of whom I speak was definitely human; I cannot deny that. But never have I witnessed or read about an individual who so valiantly desired to walk the path toward perfection for the cause of freedom from tyranny.

The journey toward perfection is what allows the raw material of humankind to rise above it all. This journey is filled with potholes, turns, curves, uphill climbs, and downhill slopes; there seems to be no real certainty to the journey, at least as the journey is being made. But in the end, this journey, should we choose to stay on its seemingly uncertain path, converts this raw material that we call humans into something more than that, perhaps even into this man of whom I speak, the father of freedom himself, George Washington, an imperfect person who did a perfect thing.

Remember that imperfect people are capable of doing perfect things, so don't wait to be perfect to make your mark. If you do, you will not amount to anything of value to society, you will never obtain your true potential (or greatness), and you will never rise above it all.

Now the question begs to be asked: "What is the gatekeeper of this journey to perfection?" The answer to the question is, of course, desire. Desire is the decision to rise above it all, whatever the sacrifice may be.

Always remember the important concept that the gatekeeper to perfection is desire. Yes, that is right. Desire is a conscious decision that must be made if transformation in its various elements is to be realized. Desire is the catalyst of action, and without it, the human experience will fall back into the destructive acts of natural phenomena. Ultimately, desire is the conscious decision to care about something bigger than yourself. The journey to greatness cannot begin without desire; those who do not possess it will have to go on various other journeys, which, in the end, will not be nearly as fulfilling. Desire is the genesis of all greatness. I will end this discussion on desire with a quote from Vince Lombardi, who said, "The difference between a successful person and others is not a lack of strength, not a lack of knowledge, but rather a lack of will," or desire.

The only prerequisite for desire is the desire to find it. If you diligently search for it, you will find it. Desire and character ultimately bring results.

Rule 2

Rule number two is that you will never become great if you are unable to appreciate the past. You will envision the greatness of your future by standing upon the shoulders of those who preceded you. Appreciation is an impossible concept in the environment of ignorance. If you want to appreciate something, you have to educate yourself, because true education ultimately brings about the realization of appreciation. If you say you are educated but you do not appreciate, then you are, in truth, not educated, just well studied.

There was a time in my life when I decided, for whatever reason, that I would study history in an effort to gain awareness and an appreciation of people around me. I decided to study the history of World War II. The following pictures will show you a little bit of what I learned about World War II.

The following picture is titled *Preparing for Death*. This picture shows men sitting in a ship and reading some literature. I believe the books they are reading are their religious scripts. Thus, they were preparing for death. This was before D-day, World War II.

Photo credit to the US National Archives and to WWII Archives

Preparing for Death

The picture below shows the soldiers coming in to the beaches of Normandy on a PT boat. Notice how curious they are as they peer over the side of this ship. One thing you should keep in mind is that at about the time this photo was taken, they were hearing the mortars going off and the shells firing at them, and they may have even been hearing shells ricocheting off their boats. This was a very nervous time for them, I'm sure. Once that PT boat opened up to let the soldiers out, many of them were killed by the flying bullets. Many others died when they jumped out of the ship and found that the ship hadn't come far enough up onto the beach. They sunk to the bottom of the ocean and drowned due to the weight of their gear.

Photo credit to the US National Archives and to WWII Archives
Soldiers Headed toward Omaha Beach on D-day

The soldiers who didn't die in the water by drowning or bullets ran up the beaches of Normandy. The operation on D-day was called Operation Overlord. Many of these soldiers were given painkillers in the form of syringes before they went up on the beach. The soldiers were told that as they ran up on the beach, they may run into land mines that could blow their limbs off. They were told that if that happened, they were to inject themselves with this painkiller and direct the other soldiers through the minefield while they died. This allowed the rest of the soldiers to continue running up the beaches of Normandy, and they did.

Photo credit to the US National Archives and to WWII Archives
Storming Normandy

While crossing the Normandy beaches, there was no cover. The soldiers were open targets for German machine guns. The lucky ones, if you want to call them that, reached the cliffs of Normandy where they could lie underneath the cliffs and have a little break from all the gunfire.

Photo credit to the US National Archives and to WWII Archives
A Shell-Shocked Soldier on the Cliffs of Normandy

The photo below is titled, *A Shell-Shocked Soldier on the Cliffs of Normandy*. This was one of the soldiers who made it to the cliffs of Normandy, where he sat down to rest. What he experienced there on that day would haunt him for the rest of his life. We should never forget this young man's face. We should never forget what other people have done to give us the gift of freedom from tyranny.

Photo credit to the US National Archives and to WWII Archives

In the end, through my studies, the soldiers of World War II came alive and became my heroes. My problem was that I never really knew any veterans from World War II. I did not come from a military family, so I was left to honor people whom I had never really met. Then one day I went to a New Year's Eve dance with my wife, Rita. We entered the dance hall and sat down by an older couple. We exchanged introductions, and my wife began a conversation with Betty, while I started a conversation with her husband, Floyd.

As the conversation with Floyd evolved, I discovered that he was a World War II veteran and that he had stormed the beaches of Normandy and fought in many of the major battles of World War II. Needless to say, I was speechless; I was sitting across the table from one of my heroes. I honestly never believed that such a day would ever arrive. I was so excited that I started investigating Floyd's role in World War II. Then his wife came over and asked to talk to me. She told me that I needed to stop talking about the war, as such conversations made it difficult for her husband to sleep at night.

I quickly apologized to Betty and went back to Floyd and talked about topics other than the war. Sometime later, my wife and I went out and shared some time on the dance floor. By the time we returned to the table, Floyd and his wife were nowhere to be found. I couldn't believe I let such an opportunity go by without expressing appreciation for this individual who I held in such high regard. In desperation, I excused myself and ran out in the parking lot hoping to find Floyd. There I saw him and his wife slowly walking across the parking lot toward their car. I ran over to Floyd and tapped him on the shoulder. He turned around and looked at me, and I finally took the opportunity to say thank you.

I eventually looked up Floyd's phone number, and the evening before Veteran's Day I asked him if he would mind dropping by and talking to my children. Floyd agreed and came by and introduced himself to my children, and then he told them a couple of stories about World War II and why they should appreciate the people who sacrificed their lives on that battlefield.

After Floyd left, I expounded on the importance of appreciating what others have sacrificed so much for. To be honest with you, I didn't think much about it after that until several months later when a friend of mine said, "Hey, John. Did you see your son's report hanging up in the entryway of the junior high school?"

The only child I had in junior high school was my eldest boy, Craig. Thanks to his mother, Craig had a respectable grade average in his schooling. However, Craig had never enjoyed reading, and as a result, I assumed that he was not much into writing either. In all sincerity, I responded back to my friend by saying, "Are you sure it was Craig's?"

He said, "Yes, and with all the reports written, his is the only one hanging in the main lobby of the school."

He recommended that I go look at it. I was certain that he must have misread his name, as I was sure that it could not have been Craig's. To make sure of these assumptions, I dropped by the school to research it for myself. I was wonderfully surprised when I walked into the school and there, right at the entrance, was the one report for everyone to see—and it was written by my son, Craig Lee. It was a report about Floyd. It is shown on the following page.

The report was simple and sweet. As you can see in the picture below, it read as follows: "Floyd, World War II veteran, was just 16 years old when he entered the service. At 18 years of age he stormed Utah beach, and fought in Normandy for world freedom. His courage and the courage of other Veterans are appreciated daily. The freedoms we all enjoy are the result of their courage."

Floyd, World War II veteran, was just 16 years old when he entered the service. At 18 years of age he stormed Utah beach, and fought in Normandy for world freedom. His courage and the courage of other Veterans are appreciated daily. The freedoms we all enjoy are the outcomes of their courage.

The Legacy and the Hero

I rushed home and asked my wife if she knew about Craig's report hanging up at the school. She told me she didn't, but she was aware of the report. My wife told me that Craig had come home and asked for help on an assignment that his teacher had given him. The report was to be about a hero of his choosing. He had chosen to write about Floyd. This was one of the proudest moments of my life!

If you ever feel lost when contemplating what around you is worthy of appreciation, remember those who were willing to give up everything so you could enjoy freedom from tyranny. Obviously there are many things around you worthy of appreciation. Pick a couple, and become an expert at those topics; this appreciation will give you the courage to rise above it all.

After you practice a bit, you will find there are reasons to appreciate things all around you, for through all written history, no one has had more to be thankful for than the people of this generation, our generation. May I repeat Isaac Newton's inspirational phrase, and I quote, "If I have seen further it is by standing on the shoulders of giants."

We all have giants from our past whose shoulders are ready to support us in our quest for greater vision; we just have to find them. Remember what was written earlier: true education will ultimately bring about the realization of appreciation; if you say you are educated but you do not appreciate, then you are, in truth, not educated, just well studied. Remember that a lack of appreciation for the past will leave you blind to opportunities of the future. You will know when you appreciate enough because the future will begin to look bright.

In my opinion, there is no greater gift that you can give to future generations than that of appreciation. The other day my wife told me that my boys were going on something called a trek and would be gone for several days. I didn't know what *trek* meant, but the boys seemed relatively excited about it, so I thought, *Well, whatever.* A few days passed, and my wife instructed me that I needed to go pick up our boys from the trek. I said, "No problem." She told me to take the truck so I would have room for all their equipment. I did as I was told, but on the way out the door, I asked her, "What is this trek anyway?" She told me the trek was where all the young people in the area would get a handcart, load it down with what would be needed to cross the plains, and push it across twenty-plus miles of desert in Wyoming along the actual pioneer trail; these young people actually traveled sixteen miles in one of those days.

On the way out the door, I thought, *Why would they be so excited to do that, especially since the last couple of days have been in the high nineties?* As I headed toward the location where I was instructed to pick up my boys, I was thinking I would meet someone in an old, rusty pickup truck where I would reload my sons' belongings into my vehicle and come home. When I got to the pickup point, I was surprised to see five tour buses of young people exiting and standing around the buses. At first I thought I must have gone to the wrong location, as this looked more like a rock concert than what I'd perceived the return from a trek would look like.

However, as I looked around, I realized that these kids (from fourteen to eighteen years old) were sun beaten and limping; that's when it hit me that this was a big deal. With all the kids around there, I was not able to find my boys right away, so for about fifteen minutes, I wandered through the crowd looking for them. It was rather inspiring to see these beat-up kids meeting up with their parents after experiencing such a journey. For the most part, the kids looked pretty bedraggled. Everyone had been browned by the sun, and all seemed to be limping from walking on blisters; some cried when they saw their parents.

Eventually I found my boys back at my truck waiting for me; they looked as beat-up as the rest. On our way home, I asked them if it was fun, and to my surprise, they said it had been. However, they admitted that it was a lot of work, as the trail went up and down hills, through mud puddles, and across rivers. They mentioned that they had even crossed an old graveyard where some pioneers had died as a result of difficulties in crossing the plains.

After a short silence, I cautiously asked them if the experience made them appreciate the pioneers more. They both responded with a confident yes, and I thought to myself, *Job well done.*

In closing, remember that you will be blind to future opportunities if you do not appreciate the past. You will never be able to effectively live a more fulfilling and productive life if you do not master the art of appreciation. The only reason the impossible is impossible is you believe it to be so. If you appreciate the past, you will see fewer impossibilities in your future.

Rule 3

You will never become greater than that which motivates you. We have already talked a fair amount about rule number three in previous chapters dealing with phase 1 behavior. In summary, if you let fear be your motivator, then the best you will ever become is average. Many people allow short-term profits to be their motivator; this will only take you and your organization so far. It has been my experience that the less you let money be your motivator, the more money you tend to receive. Henry Ford once said, "A business that makes nothing but money is a poor kind of business." Henry Ford was a very rich man.

The ultimate motivator that can lead you to the crowning achievement of human behavior (phase 3) is the desire to lift someone up, not from the desire of self-glorification but for the pure desire to lift people up and to help them succeed, even if it means the sacrifice of your own popularity.

You will find that each motivator also comes with its own unique cost or sacrifice.

Rule 4

You will never become great if you spend time blaming other people for your inability to reach greatness. If you desire pity more than greatness, then pity is what you will get. Pity and greatness are mutually exclusive characteristics.

This is a very difficult rule to learn because ultimately you will meet people who are truly victims of life's situations, and those situations demand a sense of sadness. However, for the betterment of even these people, they must gather their strength and overcome their difficulties. Sometimes a person may need to sit down with someone in confidence and just lay it all out on the table until he or she can get the monkey off his or her back, so to speak. Whatever it takes, the individual must overcome pity for his or her own situation, for it's not possible to move forward on life's journey until this event takes place.

An example of the fourth rule is Helen Keller. Helen Keller was born in 1880. At the age of two years old, she became ill, and this illness robbed her of her ability to see and hear. Ultimately, Helen Keller refused to be a victim in her own mind. Through great faith, courage, and optimism, and with a lot of sacrifice from others (for example, Miss Sullivan, her teacher), Helen Keller learned how to read, write, and communicate with the outside world. She also became a sought-after speaker worldwide. Helen Keller once said, "When one door of happiness closes, another opens, but often we look so long at the closed door that we do not see the one which has been opened for us."

I believe that all people feel a little pity for their own situations from time to time, but if you are to reach your true potential, you must learn to rise above it, or it will stop you along life's wonderful journey; in effect, pity is an anchor to progress. Think about this: the most beautiful part of life's journey lies ahead of you. Cherish the past as in the second rule, and reach for the future. You cannot do this if you allow yourself to be stuck in life's pity. Pity comes at too great a price.

Some people desire to play the role of victim, but that is different from being a victim, as it seemingly allows people to be irresponsible for the consequences of their own decisions.

Rule 5

Your ability to reach greatness is directly dependent upon the strength of your character.

As was discussed in an earlier chapter, the good news is that you can increase your character. Remember that character is the ability to follow through with a decision long after the emotions of making that decision are gone. This is a result of the relationship between sacrifice and emotions.

As mentioned earlier, when sacrifice meets emotions, emotions evaporate. And when performing tasks of value, sacrifice will always be demanded, as was illustrated in the second rule. If valuable tasks are to be performed and sustained, then character must be part of the recipe for success.

Rule 6

You cannot become great without sacrifice, and you cannot sacrifice without character.

Rule 7

You will never become great if you don't believe you can become great. You must believe. You have more potential than you know. Belief, in part, tends to be a by-product of desire.

Rule 8

You will never become great if you do not have passion for what you do. You must have passion. Passion, in part, tends to be a by-product of desire and appreciation.

Rule 9

You will never become great if you do not find within yourself the desire to serve others. If people are to rise above it all, they must learn the desire to serve others. Serving others is the ultimate motivator and will allow greatness to be realized. Don't make your life about you; make it about something bigger than you. As you do, you will discover the true nature of happiness.

Eleanor Roosevelt said it well: "Happiness is not a goal; it is a by-product."

Rule 10

You will stop becoming greater the instant you think you're great. People who think they're great never become great. I have never witnessed an exception to this rule. Once you perceive you have become great, the motive to move forward dies. Why try to become greater if you have already achieved your goal? It doesn't take a lot of achievement for most people to perceive their own greatness and destroy their ability to move forward.

Rule #10
You will stop becoming greater the instant you think you are great
(The #1 Killer of Potential)

The top peak represents true potential

"I finally made it to the peak of greatness I AM GREAT!!"

The dips symbolize the Sacrifice (evaporation of emotions) that is needed to begin the next assent ("you have to experience the fall before you can experience the rise"

The "I am Great Cloud"

Mountain of Potential

The previous figure shows the symbol for the I-Am-Great Cloud. The I-Am-Great Cloud is the number-one killer of human potential. We create the I-Am-Great Cloud by blowing up our perceived strengths so big that we can no longer see our weaknesses. This is destructive, because our weaknesses are our future strengths; without them, we cannot progress. The reason for the I-Am-Great Cloud's destructive nature is that it blinds us to our true potential and keeps us in the dark ages of human behavior.

The egocentrism of the I-Am-Great Cloud does this by promoting the false thought that we have reached the peak of greatness after a relatively mild success. We should not allow small successes to define our true potential, for if we do so, then we are simply creating an environment to nourish a destructive lie. The I-Am-Great Cloud makes the beautiful mountain of human potential look like a wall. This falsely symbolizes an ending point for human progression, when in reality, it only represents the base camp of a great and beautiful mountain of human potential. Both phase 1 and phase 2 behaviors are subject to the destructive nature of the I-Am-Great Cloud, and it is hard to rise above it all when you can't envision the next rise.

We will all experience the impact of the I-Am-Great Cloud from time to time. It is only human. If you are to rise above it all, you must learn how to create a thunderstorm in your life that will allow the blinding darkness of the I-Am-Great Cloud to dissipate, thus allowing us to envision the beauty of future opportunities. You create the thunderstorm by remembering your weaknesses. Without weaknesses and the recognition of weaknesses, it would be impossible to rise above it all, because you stop becoming greater the instant you think you are great. Everyone needs a rainy day from time to time.

After the I-Am-Great Cloud dissipates, the beauty of the mountain of human potential may be overwhelmed by the sacrifice needed to reach the next visible peak. This perceived sacrifice may exceed your current level of character, and it is likely you will slide down the curve and bottom out before you begin your next ascent. Remember that you must experience the fall before you can experience the rise. You may climb and fall several times before successfully finding your next peak. You shouldn't worry though; this is only natural. If you will leave scratch marks every time you fall down and claw your way to new heights, then eventually your character will increase to the extent that the next peak will be obtainable. Of course, when you reach your next peak, the I-Am-Great Cloud will grow dark again. The reason for the darkness is that your new accomplishments make you feel great again. Most things in life have a purpose, and perhaps the I-Am-Great Cloud has a purpose also. Perhaps the I-Am-Great Cloud allows you to rest and gain the necessary strength to reach the next summit.

So perhaps the I-Am-Great Cloud is only destructive if we lack the skill to create the needed Thunderstorm. A more controllable way of creating the thunderstorm is to always read about the lives of individuals who have climbed higher peaks than where you currently reside. Another excellent way, and perhaps less painful, is to appreciate the past. Remember that appreciating the past allows us to envision a more fulfilling future. Appreciation is capable of creating the thunderstorm, which, in turn, allows us to see the next peak. The most painful elements used to create the thunderstorm are the use of shame and guilt. Shame and guilt will create the thunderstorm but are incapable of allowing you to reach your true potential; you will never become greater than that which motivates you, and shame and guilt are lower-level motivators. So in short, the appreciation methodology is preferred over the shame and guilt procedure.

Because phase 1 behavior is motivated by fear, guilt, and shame, it has limited capability of climbing the beautiful mountain of human behavior. Phase 2 is motivated by the thoughts of self-glorification, so it is also has limited capability of climbing the mountain of human potential because it will quickly create the I-Am-Great Cloud. Phase 3 is motivated by the purest of motives and, therefore, is capable of guiding you to the higher peaks of human potential. Phase 3 also allows people to help guide other people up the mountain of human potential. It would be very difficult to climb the mountain without the guidance of phase 3 behavior. The big problem is we need more phase 3 behavior. There are only as many phase 3 organizations as there are phase 3 leaders.

In closing, I must say we have talked about how we can create a thunderstorm to temporarily get rid of the I-Am-Great Cloud.

Rule 11

You will never become great if you are afraid to fail. If you let fear of failure motivate your actions, the best you will ever become is average.

Rule 12

Patience—you must have patience, for every great destiny has a specific journey. Lack of patience will cause you to attempt a shortcut on that journey, which may not allow the destiny to be realized. One of the important ingredients in rising above it all is patience. The element of patience that you must be most concerned with is the patience you exercise toward yourself. Remember that we all start at the bottom of the model (phase I); evolving takes time. Enjoy the journey, for when all else is done, what else is there to enjoy but the memories of that journey?

Rule 13

You will never become great if you are unable to focus on what is important. I have been fairly involved in high-risk sports for the majority of my life. Unfortunately, I have had friends die while participating in these activities. I have nearly died on several occasions myself. One of my near-death experiences took place during the early spring months when I was jumping at a drop zone located in the heart of the Rocky Mountains. It was a beautiful place and a beautiful day.

On this particular day, I had left my wrist-mounted altimeter back at my apartment, so instead of driving back, I just borrowed a chest-mounted altimeter from the drop zone. An altimeter is used to tell skydivers what their altitude is—in other words, how high up in the air they are. The jumpers have a targeted deployment altitude, so they know when to deploy their parachute. The deployment target is usually around three thousand feet. The goal is to watch your altimeter to know when it's time to deploy.

The first jump I made that day was a solo jump. During that jump, the altimeter blew under my chin, and I could not see it during free fall, so I simply deployed early. I went back to the drop zone and attempted to fix the problem. With the new alteration to the altimeter, I got back on the plane and performed another solo jump. The new alteration did not work, so I played it safe and performed a slightly early deployment again. Nothing is more agonizing to an experienced skydiver than a long, boring ride under canopy. When I arrived back at the drop zone, I performed some other procedures to the altimeter. At that time, some of my buddies came up and invited me to participate in some relative work. Relative work is where several skydivers get together, jump out of the plane, and create formations such as shapes of stars and triangles. I was excited to have the opportunity to have a lot of fun with my friends, so we jumped in the plane and off we went.

During our ascent to jump altitude (approximately ten thousand feet), I told my friends about the problem I'd been having with my altimeter and asked them to let me know when we had reached deployment altitude, which was approximately three thousand feet for this particular jump. They came up with a signal they would use to communicate when deployment altitude was reached. We all practiced it, and once we reached jump altitude, we bailed out of the plane together. As we accelerated to the ground, we began creating our formations in the sky. We had a lot of fun!

On our last formation before deployment altitude, one of the jumpers got separated from the group. Just as we approached deployment altitude, the missing jumper closed the gap and bumped into the side of me. As a result of this mild collision, I went tumbling out into the wild, blue sky. Now I must tell you that about every three months or so I received a skydiving magazine in the mail. In the back of this magazine was a very important report titled, "Fatality Reports." It would always contain the latest fatalities in the sport. It was published in an effort to educate skydivers on how to save their lives in difficult situations.

The fatality report would always go over the incident and then explain what the skydiver could have done differently to avoid the fatality. In a recent report, I remember reading about a group of people doing relative work, which is exactly what my friends and I were doing. Somehow one of the skydivers fell below the rest of the team and then, around deployment altitude, deployed per their plan. Little did the diver know that there was one individual still in free fall right above him.

After the lower jumper deployed, the one above him fell right into the deployed parachute; as a result, both members of the team died after violently crashing into the ground. Within the skydiving community, this is called bouncing. You probably don't want to know why they use that terminology.

Before continuing my free-fall story, I must define a phenomena referred to as ground rush. When you are falling from an airplane, it actually feels like you are floating until you get somewhere below 1,500 feet at which time you can visually recognize that the earth is rapidly accelerating toward you. We refer to this phenomena as ground rush. My experience suggests that ground rush creates adrenaline rush.

So back to my free-fall story. I quickly realized the potential danger and decided to free-fall to the point when if someone above me waited any longer, they would have waited too long. So I decided that I would watch the ground until I felt ground rush; then I would give it a second or two count and deploy.

From the many fatality reports I have studied and learned from, I was aware of a couple of other dangerous phenomena. The most dangerous one was that some people become fixated on what would kill them, such as the ground, and never focus on what could save them. The result of this phenomenon, of course, is death. I know this to be true, because I once had a friend with whom I shared an evening jump in Northern California, and the next day I came back and was told she had died earlier in the day. She was in a situation similar to mine, and when she started experiencing ground rush, she couldn't think about anything but the danger. As a result, she bounced. Lesson learned—focus on what can save, not on what destroys.

With regards to me, I began to experience the ground rush. I was so close to the ground at this point that I could see a car cruising down the road, and I could see the driver inside. I can still remember turning my attention away from the ground and focusing all my efforts on what could save me. I remember watching my hand as if it were in slow motion as I reached for my pilot chute, grabbed the knob, pulled the pilot chute out of the pocket, and threw it out into the wind stream—resulting in a successful deployment of the parachute.

I used all my energy concentrating on my body position in hopes that the deployment would be both efficient and effective. Ultimately, everything went as hoped, and the deployed parachute slowed me down just as I hit the ground. My timing was perfect—not a second to spare!

The owners of the drop zone had been watching the jump and noticed several deployments at the horizon line of the mountain, and then they saw a dot (me) drop well into the mountain range before the successful deployment. They thought I was going to die. They were always proud of the fact that they had never had a fatality. Needless to say, they were not happy with me when I got to the ground.

As a person who participated in high-risk activities, I had plenty of things I needed to work on, but one strength I naturally had was that when circumstances evolved into dangerous situations, I naturally keep my awareness of the danger but focus my energy on what had the potential to save me. This skill has saved my life on several occasions. If you do not develop this skill in the competitive world of business, then you leave your organization at risk of extinction. You must learn to do the same thing in your personal life if you are to experience a more fulfilling and productive life.

One of the phenomena I have noticed in organizations that put off transformation until it is too late and they are about to fall into extinction is that they are focused on what will kill them instead of what could save them. These dying organizations focus mostly on the personify, blame, and punish methodology, which was the biggest reason for their soon-to-be extinction, instead of focusing on systems thinking, which could have saved them. In reality, the evolving of the personify, blame, and punish phenomena makes sense in such an environment, because when an organization is about to become extinct, the pressure becomes so great that individuals snap and slide down the curve to lower levels of behavior where the preferred problem-solving methodology is personify, blame, and punish.

In summary, remember to focus on that which can save the organization and don't get hypnotized by what can destroy it. When I use the word *organization* in this context, it could be a business or it could be your family. Also remember that every organization and person has a unique level of character, and after that level is exceeded, the organization or individual will slide into lower levels of behavior. The most common reason for organizations and people to exceed their level of character is managers or people asking themselves to perform more than they are capable of, at least at that moment of time.

Organizations should have two visions—a published vision and an unpublished vision. The published vision should not overload the organizational capacity. Remember that every organization has its own unique level of character, and after it is exceeded, it will slide into lower levels of behavior and practice personify, blame, and punish. You must be aware of danger but not intently focused on it. The skydiving analogy is that people become mesmerized by the ground rush to the point that they freeze up. We do need to be aware of where the ground is, but we should focus on the deployment mechanism. Focus on that which can save!

Rule 14

Remember to never ever, ever, ever, ever give up! You can do it! I once taught a Six Sigma Green Belt class for a client. The objective of the class was to prepare the students for a very difficult national certification exam. The pass rate on this type of exam was somewhere between 60 percent and 70 percent. After the class, I was very satisfied that of the twenty students, only one had failed. That is a pass rate of approximately 95 percent—much higher than the national average.

From my many failures in life, I have always tried to learn something from each of them. One of the things I have learned is to not forget the one. In other words, go ahead and celebrate with the nineteen, but when it is all over, don't forget the one. The supervisor of this student (the student's name was Adam) sent me a letter telling me how devastated Adam was being the only one among his peers who failed the exam. In the letter, the supervisor told me Adam was going to give up, as failure was just too painful for him. The supervisor asked me if there was anything I could do to help Adam keep from feeling so bad and to talk him into not giving up.

In response, I wrote something similar to the following:

Dear Adam,

I heard that you struggled on the green belt exam. Please don't feel bad—many people have to take these exams more than once. I have also failed certification exams, more than once, so I just keep moving along and retaking them until I pass them. I had one student take the certification exam seven times before he passed it. After all was said and done, the student told me he was glad he didn't pass it the first time, as he learned more and more each time he took the exam. In the end, it is about learning, so don't give up. Knowledge comes at a price, and everyone has their own price. The great WB Dubois once said "Toil stands before the gates of knowledge." Don't compare your price to other people's prices. The price other people have to pay for knowledge is no one else's business. Comparing your price to others can be very destructive in reaching your true potential.

I don't tell many people this, but I used to be in resource mathematics when I was in junior high school. In fact, I never really understood mathematics until I continued my studies after high school, as I will explain later. No one seemed overly concerned as they just realized that I wasn't all that smart. Unfortunately for me, I always enjoyed learning, but learning was very difficult for me. I started my educational career in the Head Start Program. From what I understand that was a program for high-risk children. I'm not sure who determines high risk; I never felt I was high risk. I remember in junior high school a teacher by the name of Mrs. Ransom who decided she was going to teach me math. There were only two of us in her class. (Most would have considered us the two dumbest students in the school.)

Mrs. Ransom was a very successful teacher, who would always remember the "one." In this case, I was the "one." Every day she would try to teach me the principles of mathematics and every day I would fail; eventually she had to let me go as I moved on into high school. After high school I started studying a simplified mathematics and physics book called *The Nature of Automotive Dynamics* by Steve Smith. It was a technical book about race cars. I found the book just the other day as I was cleaning up my office. It fell off the bookshelf onto the floor and the pages went everywhere—what a mess it made! When I saw it, I was ashamed, as it reminded me of how dumb I was. I quickly bent down and picked up all the pages and stuffed them back into the book. You see, there was a reason why all those pages fell out. I would read that book everywhere I went. I took it to the factory with me, and during breaks I would read it; I would read it at stoplights, and I would read it before and after work. At the end of each reading I realized I did not understand any of its contents. That's right, nothing—zero.

I knew that everything came at a price, and the price of knowledge for me was extremely high. It was all right though; I kept reading it anyway. Sometimes I would get teased for reading that book so often, especially when people would ask me what it was about and I would have to tell them I didn't know.

Anyway, I kept reading this book for literally years. After about twenty reads, I still didn't understand it, but on the twenty-first time, yes, on the twenty-first time, it all made sense to me. I couldn't believe it; I understood everything in the book. I had to understand it in my own way, an easier way, but I didn't see anything wrong with that; in fact it helped me understand it in a way that allowed me to understand it deeper than others. To me it was miraculous—the floodgates had finally opened. I would go to the local racetrack (where I raced stock cars) and listen to the engineers talk about automotive dynamics. I understood everything they said and even recognized their misunderstandings of the concepts (eventually I authored the book *The Nature of Dynamic Weight Transfer*). I didn't argue with them, as I lacked the credibility to do so. This new understanding had a great impact on me. It made me believe that, maybe, just maybe, I wasn't dumb after all—well, and at least not as dumb as I thought I was. In fact, I started to think that perhaps, just perhaps, I was smart enough to go to college.

However, no one else felt I was smart enough to go to college—except, of course, my mother. Thank God everyone is given a mother. Although it took me a lot longer than most others, eventually I graduated from university as a mechanical engineer. I was never the smartest student, but I was always the hardest-working student. The apartment complex where I lived as a student once handed out awards for people in the complex. I won the award for the person who spent the most time in the library. I was waiting at the library entrance when the janitor unlocked the door, and I only left when they announced over the intercom that it was time to lock up. I would read some of my assignments on audiotape and I would listen to them over and over again, all in hopes of scoring in the middle of the class. And yes, I had plenty of critics through the whole experience. I was so proud when I was going to graduate as a mechanical engineer; it was only days away and I could not believe I had finally pulled it off. To me graduation was more than just a goal it was a goal with a heartbeat. I call goals with heartbeats dreams. And graduating from the university with a degree in mechanical engineering had a healthy heartbeat. That heartbeat is what kept me in the library all the time.

I wish I could tell you that somehow I became smarter. The reality of the situation is that I did not. I still understand things in simplified ways. When I listen to a lecture I still have to reconsider it in a way that is simpler. As a result most things around me look simple perhaps simpler than they really are—I am not sure about that. Ultimately I found that people like me to teach them my simplistic way of viewing difficult to understand topics. My weakness became my strength. Remember that effort is the hammer, weakness is the raw material, and the output is strength. You can't create the output if you are missing any of the inputs. Weaknesses are essential to the plan.

So anyway, if you desire to pass the test, step up and don't give up—no matter how many times it takes. If it is not something you are interested in, then I understand that also. Mostly, I just wanted to tell you not to feel bad about not passing the test.

Thanks,
John Lee
President of Alpha Training and Consulting
BSME, MBA, CMQ/OE, CQE, CRE, CQA, CQIA, CQI, CCT, CQPA, CQT, CHA, CBA, CSQE, CSSGB, CSSBB, AQC Six Sigma Master BB
www.alphaTC.com

He responded 0with something like the following letter:

John,

Thank you so much. I really appreciate you taking the time to send me this e-mail. It is inspiring and very kind. I will take the test again. I am going to join a study group and take it in October.

Thank you so much for all your help.

So to you readers out there, don't forget the fourteenth rule of greatness, and please, never give up on yourself or others. If you do, you will never know your true potential. Remember that we are in the dark ages of your true potential.

Remember that to become great is to change. Winston Churchill once said, "To improve is to change—to become perfect is to change often."

In the most difficult and discouraging days of World War II, Winston Churchill said to the people of England, "To every man there comes that special moment when he is, figuratively, tapped on the shoulder and offered the chance to do a special thing unique to him and fitted to his talent. What a tragedy if that moment finds him unprepared or unqualified for the work which would be his finest hour."

Don't ever stop preparing for that finest hour that, without doubt, will someday manifest itself to you. I know, because I have felt that figurative tap on my shoulder.

Prepare to make a difference; once prepared, you will know what to do from there.

Chapter Five

Living a Productive Life

One of the rules of transformation lies at the center of living a more productive life. The rule is that you will never become greater than that which motivates you.

We spend a significant amount of our life working. I suspect everyone works—at least, everyone I know works. Sometimes people ask me if my wife works. My response is "yes, she works in the home." In fact, oftentimes she works harder than I do. The point being that we all spend a significant part of our lives working. So if work is not fulfilling, then our goal of living a more fulfilling and productive life is in jeopardy. From my experiences in life, it is hard to make work fulfilling if we are not productive. This chapter of the book is dedicated to creating a purpose-based reason for going to work.

One of the reasons for organizational existence is to create wealth in an efficient and effective manner. For nonprofit organizations, one of the reasons for organizational existence is to use wealth more efficiently and effectively to reach the organization's objectives. Most people do not understand the importance of wealth creation. Everyone who works should understand why wealth creation is important. It is through the creation of wealth that opportunity for future generations is created. This desire to create wealth will ultimately evolve into a higher motivator that will allow us the power to transform the way we approach work.

If wealth is such an important concept, I'd probably be wise to define it. So what is wealth? Wealth is an abundance of those things that we value. It can often, but not always, be effectively measured in monetary units, such as dollars. One of the more common measurements of wealth is how many widgets we can make per person in our society. In the world of transformation, a widget has a specific definition. A widget is defined as a product or service that improves the human condition.

So what happens when you create more widgets per person in society? Hypothetically, if we create more widgets per person, then the human condition should improve, because widgets improve the human condition. Therefore, if we were to make more of them, it should naturally improve the human condition—this is a key concept.

Let me give you an example of using higher motives and how it works. When I am traveling around, I often listen to the radio and look at the billboards along the highway as a method of staying alert. In doing so, I always found one advertising campaign more interesting than most. The company was the Workmen's Compensation Fund of Utah (WCF). From what I understand, WCF is an insurance company of sorts, so it obviously has a financial interest in workers' safety on the job. I witnessed the WCF's various advertising campaigns over the years but didn't pay a lot of attention to them until one day I was speeding down the highway (a bad habit I have always had) and noticed a new billboard. It displayed a picture of a cute little kid standing in a construction zone with a sign in his hand that read: "Daddy, please come home tonight. I need you." I immediately dropped my speed down by about ten miles per hour. It turns out this advertisement not only had an impact on me but was an extremely successful advertising campaign to bring a higher level of safety awareness to the citizenry of Utah. My point is that you will never become greater than that which motivates you, so be sure to choose your motives carefully, because they are of strategic importance. Therefore, if you can tie the reason you go to work with the well-being of generations of your family, then you are more likely to work from higher motives. These higher motives are what make work more fulfilling.

Now for a story about the importance of creating wealth or using wealth wisely. This story takes place in the Dark Ages of Europe. The Dark Ages of Europe in the Middle Ages was a period in history considered by many to be a time when there was very little social, artistic, or scientific advancement. In fact, not only was there no significant advancement, but on many fronts society progressed extremely slowly in the Dark Ages.

This period of history started with the decline of the Roman Empire and lasted until the European cultural transformation that is often referred to as the Renaissance. Most historians consider this time period of the Middle Ages between AD 410 and AD 1400 as the Dark Ages. If you dislike change, then perhaps these times in the past were for you.

Before you decide to fantasize about the beauty and lack of change of these times, perhaps we should take a look at this time period until after the industrial revolution in the nineteenth century in greater depth. During these times before social changes were made, one-half of the children died before they reached adulthood, and one-quarter of the children died as newborns. Most children would lose one or both parents before they reached adulthood. People wore their clothes until the clothes rotted off their backs. Suddenly, the past without change doesn't seem so great, does it? But you haven't heard anything yet!

Something else about these past times is that there were not a lot of opportunities. Because of the feudal society, children pretty much did what their parents did. Most of the people were malnourished, and public education was only for the children of wealthy families. Without education, there was no real way for advancement in life, and life was all about survival.

I read through some family journals and found a story about a young girl born during dark times in Fife, Scotland. The child was one of my ancestors and was born into a family of coal miners, called coaliers at that time. The word later evolved into what we call today *colliers*. This story is about me, and ultimately, you will find it is about you also. The name of the girl in the family history story is Margaret. I was rather shocked when I learned that all her family members were essentially slaves in the coal mines. During this time period, there was a high demand for coal. The coal was used to dry sea salt, and there weren't enough people who were willing to stay around and work in the coal mines. It wasn't exactly a fun job! Because they could not sustain a labor force to work in these mines, the coal mine owners took the people who knew how to mine coal and made them slaves. The parliament in Fife,

Scotland, basically made slavery legal, and whole families worked in the coal mines as property of the mine owners.

Often the parents would go down into the coal pit and knock coal from the walls. The children would then pick up the coal in buckets and carry these coal-filled buckets up ladders where they would be stockpiled for the community. The family would usually work six days a week, fourteen hours a day. The children were referred to as "coal bearers." School and education were nothing but a pipe dream. Legal and social degradation by many acts of the Scotland parliament caused the rest of the population to look upon the miners or colliers as something less than human. They were herded together in miserable hovels and villages close to the pits. In Fife, a dead collier was not allowed to be buried in the same ground as a free laborer. It was a rather sad situation. During my reading of the family history, I came across this letter from a young girl with the name of Margaret Levitston. (Levitston later became Livingston, my great-grandmother's maiden name.) She was a coal bearer and carried the buckets of coal out of the mine. She wrote:

> "**Been down the pit at coal carrying for six weeks – make 10-14 journeys a day. Carriers a full 56 lbs. of coal in a wooden backit. The work is no gaid: it is so vary sair. I work with sister Jesse and mother: dinna ken the time we gang it is gae dark. Get plenty of broth and porridge and run home and get a bannock. Never been to school it is so very far away.**"

Notice that there appears to be many misspelled words. This is not the case. The words are written as the Scottish dialect is spoken in their language. I'm going to try to interpret the letter for you. This is what it says: "Been down in the coal pit for six weeks—make 10–14 journeys a day. Carry a full 56 lbs. of coal in a wooden basket. The work is no good; it is very painful. I work with sister Jesse and Mother: I don't know the time we went (home), it is getting dark. Get plenty of broth and porridge and run home and get a bannock. Never been to school; it is so very far away."

Well, school *was* far away. I'm sure it was far away geographically, but it was an eternity away. From Margaret's letter I sensed a strong desire to go to school, but as I said earlier, these people had zero opportunity to improve their situation.

Something obviously happened between that time and the time I am living in today, because I have more opportunity than I have time to take advantage of it—a deep contrast compared to the life Margaret lived. I will now tell you a story to try to help you understand what may have happened.

This is the story. One day these colliers' lives were about to change drastically as a direct result of a gentleman who came to the mine and explained to the mine owners that he could hook up a conveyor system powered by a water wheel or animal power (whichever they preferred), and this power could be used to haul the buckets of coal out of the mine. He explained that by using this new mechanism, they could send all the coal miners home except for the fathers. The mine owners decided to give the man a chance to prove out his idea. The idea worked! The machine could pull coal out of the mine with fewer people. The next day the mine owners called all the colliers together and told them about this new mechanism and how they could haul coal out of the mine with this machine. They announced to the workers that the only people who would be allowed to continue their labor in the coal mine were the fathers.

As a result of this conveyor system, all the other workers were laid off except for the fathers. What do you think? Do you think they were happy with this layoff? Imagine that! They no longer had to go to these dreadful coal mines. It turns out that most of the workers were very depressed. Why? Why would people be depressed if they didn't have to go to that dreadful coal mine anymore? Well, one of the obvious reasons was so they could feed their families, but beyond that, there's something unique about human beings—they desire to participate and make a difference. They desire to have a fulfilling life. The only way these people knew how to participate in society was to dig coal. Also, they lost the short-term ability to work for their food. The miners felt that the rug had been pulled out from under them; when they could no longer participate, they felt discouraged and depressed.

So back at the coal mine, everyone was pretty discouraged and depressed except for one man, who was somewhat of a visionary and was also Margaret's father. Margaret's father called her to his side, knelt down on his knees, and looked into his daughter's coal-stained face. He then told Margaret that this was the greatest day in all his life. He told her that he never dared dream of having a daughter who would not have to live and die in the dreadful coal mines. He also told Margaret that he had a plan, and he needed her to help him realize this dream. Margaret agreed to do all that she could to help with her father's plan.

He then told Margaret that instead of going to the coal mine the next morning, she should go to Isaac's house. Isaac was a neighbor who lived some distance down the street, and she was to go and work there. He told Margaret that she must work fourteen-hour days, six days a week at Isaac's house (the same hours she worked in the coal mine). She was instructed to sweep Isaac's walks, wash his windows, take care of the cattle, mend fences, and fix whatever else appeared to be in need of repair. Margaret's father told her that it may take a while, but she was to continue working on Isaac's property until she found favor with Isaac. She was then instructed by her father that it was extremely important that as soon as she gained favor with Isaac, she was to excuse herself from her labors and run to the coal mine and find him, because he would be anxiously waiting to give her further directions.

The next morning at around four o'clock, Margaret was awakened by her father. For the first time since Margaret had begun working in the mines at six years of age, Margaret took a different path than her father. Not only did she take a different direction physically, but idealistically the girl's life was about to change relative to her father's. Margaret went to Isaac's house, and her father returned to the coal mines. Margaret did as her father instructed and worked six days a week, fourteen hours a day taking care of Isaac's property. Several weeks went by, and Margaret was faithful to her father's plan.

Then early one afternoon, Isaac came out on his porch and looked around at his property. He was amazed at how great it looked. He had been watching Margaret for some time and greatly respected the young girl's work ethic. Ultimately, Isaac called Margaret over and told her he had never seen his property look so good. He told Margaret he would like to reward her for her hard work. He asked her, "Would you like some candy? Would you like some clothes?" (You have to remember that the colliers would wear their clothes until they rotted from their backs.) "Or perhaps some money? What can I do for you, Margaret, for all the service that you have provided me?" Throughout the whole conversation, Margaret realized or recognized that this was her cue to go back and speak with her father. Margaret asked Isaac if she may be excused, because she needed to talk with her father. Isaac laughed at the indecisive young girl and said that she could come back whenever she was ready to claim her reward.

Margaret had never been so excited in all her life. She felt that she had truly succeeded. She knew that her father would be so very proud of her. Margaret ran as fast as she could to the coal pit and scooted down the ladder as fast as she could. From there, she ran into the depths of the coal mine where she found her father literally slaving away in a dark corner of the pit. Margaret looked at her father with a big smile on her now coal-stained face and told him, "Father, I have found favor with Isaac!"

Margaret's father ran over to his daughter and fell to his knees. Margaret had never witnessed her father cry before and felt a little bit nervous. With tears of optimism running down his face, Margaret's father looked into his little girl's coal-stained face and told her, "This is the greatest day in our lives! This is what I want you to do. You must go back to Isaac and ask him if he wouldn't mind attempting to teach a poor little collier girl how to read."

Filled with her father's optimism, Margaret ran back to Isaac's home and knocked on his door. As Margaret heard footsteps approach the door, she began to be afraid. What if Isaac rejected her request? She was afraid that would crush her father for life. She knew people were prejudiced against the colliers. What if Isaac didn't feel that Margaret even had the potential to read? That was the way many people felt back then. It was not hard to see the gravity of the moment and how disappointed her father would be if this didn't work out.

After what seemed like an eternity, the door opened slowly, and there was Isaac standing at the door. In an intimidating voice, Isaac asked, "Well, girl, what is it?"

With all the courage a young girl could muster, she looked right into Isaac's eyes and quietly and sincerely asked him, "Would you mind attempting to teach a little peasant girl, even a collier girl, how to read?"

To Margaret's disbelief, Isaac smiled, stretched out his hand, patted the young girl on the head, and told her, "I would be honored to attempt to teach a poor little peasant girl—even a collier girl—how to read."

With Margaret's heart pounding, she followed Isaac into his kitchen, where she was instructed to sit down at his dinner table. Isaac then went to another room, got a book, sat down by the girl, and began the miraculous act of teaching the poor little collier girl how to read.

At the same time Margaret was finishing up her first reading lesson, her father arrived home from the mine. He was very nervous when he realized that his daughter had not returned home. Finally he could wait no longer and started walking down the long road toward Isaac's house. As he reached the midpoint in his travels, he noticed the dark shadow of a little girl with her hair bouncing up and down in an expression of her excitement. With his heart about to break, the next thing her father knew, his daughter was flying into his open arms. Hugs were exchanged as her father gained the courage to ask the question of her success or failure. When Margaret yelled out, "He is teaching me how to read!" the excitement ripped all the strength from the young father, and they fell to the ground in celebration of their good fortune.

As the years went by, Margaret's father became ill with black lung disease and was on his deathbed. He decided to look out the shack's window one last time before slipping away into what he hoped would be a better tomorrow. In the far distance, he noticed an individual walking down the road. He saw that it was a woman with a book in her hand. Back then, having a book in your hand really meant something—it suggested that you could read, and that demanded respect from all those around you. If you could read, people would listen to you and believe you. You were a respectable person if you knew how to read.

As the image grew closer to the father's fading vision, he noticed that it was his daughter. It was Margaret! Shortly after that proud moment, Margaret's father died in his daughter's loving arms. He died that day with one of the greatest gifts in his heart—the gift of knowing that his life had made a difference.

The important question to ask and for you to answer is what was the nucleus or central event that allowed Margaret the opportunity to read?

This event was the gentleman coming to the mine and setting up the conveyor belt to haul coal out of the mine. It was the layoffs. Why? Because the mechanism allowed society to create more widgets per person, and remember that a widget is a product or service that improves the human condition. And it indeed improved the human condition in Margaret's life and also mine!

After the change, the mine was capable of fulfilling society's need for coal with fewer people. In doing so, the act created what we call opportunity. There's no such thing as opportunity as we know it without the creation of wealth. Thus, the creation of wealth becomes an extremely important activity. By creating wealth more efficiently, we too can make a difference in not only our own lives but perhaps more importantly in the lives of our children and our children's children. And perhaps someday someone, perhaps many years from now, will stand up and tell a story about your life and how your sacrifices created a better life.

Eventually the colliers gained their freedom from the owners of the mine, but many of them continued to mine as the demand for coal continued to increase. Eventually some received a call in their hearts—a call of freedom to go to another land and start a new life. Many of them came to the United States and helped start the US mining industry. But Margaret's great-grandchild, many generations down the line, James, came to America. At a very young age (grade-school age), he worked in the granite quarries. Eventually James grew up and ran the granite quarry; there is now a plaque there that honors his sacrifices (one of his arms was blown off by dynamite). Every morning when I wake up I see the granite quarry from my front window, and I remember Margaret and her descendants' sacrifices and how they have impacted my life. I go to work every day and work my hardest in an effort to pass on the blessings of those sacrifices, and more if possible, to my children in hopes that someday I too will make a difference. And what exactly am I trying to do to make this difference? I try to create more widgets per person every day, with every breath, so I may be the author of opportunity for others yet unknown.

Memorial to James Livingston

Remember that perfection is a journey not a destiny. This journey takes longer than one lifetime; the journey is a family affair. Don't give up.

My point is this: at the end of the day, we have very little except for those things that other people have given us from the results of their sacrifices. So the third rule of fulfillment and productivity is this: you will never realize a future that you cannot envision, and you cannot envision a better future without an appreciation for the past.

I have a difficult time finding a more destructive element in the world of fulfillment than fear. Fear is a reflection of a loss of hope. Sadly, most people are motivated by fear, and where there is fear, there is no hope. The point is that you can't obtain a better future without the hope of a better future. I feel that the real cause of general fear in society, and in our own personal lives, is a lack of appreciation for the past. Fear is destructive enough to destroy the greatest economies in the world. It is also powerful enough to destroy the greatest organizations in the world, including yours.

If you cannot appreciate the past, you cannot envision a better future. In other words, if you cannot appreciate the past, you will fear the future.

Oh, what the world could be if only we could master the art of appreciation! Great people have usually mastered the art of appreciation. Remember what Isaac Newton said: "If I have seen further it is by standing on the shoulders of giants." We can all stand on the shoulders of giants. We must learn who those giants are, and we must learn to appreciate them. By doing so, we will master the art of appreciation just as Isaac Newton did, and just like Isaac Newton, we will see farther than most.

I spend a fair amount of time teaching about the art of appreciation in an effort to help people discover fulfillment. I tell my students that they will know they have appreciated enough when the future looks bright again. If we, as a generation of Americans, feel that we do not have anything to be thankful for, then no one in all of written history had anything to be thankful for, for no one has had more opportunity than we have. Sometimes people, myself included, act like these are the worst times in all of history. I have read history, and these are not the worst of times, relatively speaking. These are the best of times, and the only reason we see them as anything but that is our inability to appreciate the past and our motive of fear. Run an experiment by taking a day and attempting to appreciate all you are capable of imagining. When you are full of appreciation, look into the future and see if it looks brighter than it did the day before. It will because the I-Am-Great Cloud will have had a thunderstorm.

After I lecture on the art of appreciation, it is not unusual to see individuals working their way through the crowd so they can visit with me. Ultimately, these people will tell me life stories to help express their appreciation for what they have. To date, these people who come and tell me their stories come from a single demographic group. Can you guess what group that is? They always come from the demographic group of immigrants. Ultimately, they tell me they are appreciative of their humble beginnings, which allow them to appreciate what they have. I have found that appreciation is like salt; as salt enhances a meal, so appreciation enhances all human experiences.

Wealth without appreciation does not necessarily create happiness; again, appreciation enhances all the human experiences. Wealth creation has the potential of creating opportunity only when it is enhanced with the ingredient of appreciation.

Remember that life is like a book, and you only get to write one of them; you are the only one authorized to write it, so let's make it a great one.

I have one client who manufactures medical devices. The company workers go to the hospital every year and visit patients to see them use the devices that they are instrumental in creating. This brings the employees a sense of purpose greater than money. So always remember: you will never become greater than that which motivates you.

And finally, don't forget your preferred motives. Go to work and create opportunities for future generations. Look around you and figure out how you can create more widgets per person. Remember that it is your legacy.

So what is the outcome of a successful personal transformation to higher motives? You will have the ability to envision a better future, and you will be going to work for the right reason. Work will be filled with purpose, and your motives will be to create more widgets per person. Why? So you can create opportunity for those who follow you. In other words, you will go to work to create opportunity for future generations just like past generations did for you. After the personal transformation, you will be filled with passion and the desire to make a difference in the world. Always remember that we will never become greater than that which motivates us.

Chapter Six

A Life Worth Living

Imagine how difficult it would be to live a fulfilling and productive life if you do not have a deep sense of the value of your life.

The objective of this chapter is to help you more deeply understand the value of the life experience. There are many reasons why an individual may undervalue the worth of his or her life. One of these reasons may be that the person values life based on the perception of closeness to perfection. The logic is based off the thought that the more perfect a person is the more valuable that person's life is. This would make sense if you considered perfection to be a destiny instead of a journey. If you look at perfection as a journey, then it is easier to understand the true value of life.

I will use a story to help you understand my reasoning for putting such a high value on the life experience.

I will start the story as all great stories start: once upon a time.

Once upon a time I decided to spend my spring break from college going to a skydiving party in the great state of Arizona. In the skydiving community, they call these parties boogies. I am not certain where the term boogie came from, but wherever it came from, it stuck and you can attend boogies all over the world if you have the resources and desire to do so. I really enjoyed going to the Arizona Easter Boogie because it was relatively close to the university that I attended, but perhaps, more importantly, it got me out of the cold, snow-clad Rocky Mountains. An added benefit is that I was able to do a lot of skydiving with a lot of fun people.

After my arrival, I went to the heart of the boogie, which I refer to as the tent community. The tent community is where everyone gathers for social purposes as well as planning their upcoming jumps. It's also where people set up their tents. From my initial surveillance, I suspect there were more than a thousand people in the tent community. I also noticed a large lineup of relatively large airplanes on the grounds of the airport. From my observations, I was anticipating a very fun weekend.

As I was walking through the crowds, I noticed that a significant number of people were gathered around one person. I later learned that his name was Jesse. As I walked by, I must admit I was wondering what made him so special. Upon further investigation, I discovered his full name was Jesse Carson, and he was the most accomplished skydiver in the country. They no doubt paid him to attend the event.

I have never been the type of person to chase down famous people. It just wasn't that big of a deal to me, so I walked past the crowd of people and stopped to watch a video that was being presented on how to do some interesting relative work. After enjoying the learning session, I sat down at a table and ordered a drink. To my surprise, Jesse came up and asked if he could join me. Of course, I had to say yes. I couldn't pass up such a unique opportunity.

As we talked, I realized that Jesse was much different from my initial perceptions. I just assumed he would be the type of person who was full of himself. I turned out to be completely wrong. After talking for a short period of time, I found he was extremely interested in me, and I sat around talking about myself for more than an hour. I hate to admit it, but I actually enjoyed the time I spent with Jesse and secretly hoped that we could become close friends. That thought quickly left my mind as I saw all the people surround him as soon as he left my table. As he walked away, I realized that Jesse was different from most people I knew. Somewhere deep inside I could understand why everyone was following Jesse around.

As the afternoon evolved into evening, I was able to meet with old friends and meet a few new ones. I eventually joined a group of skydivers who planned a jump that we would perform the next morning (Saturday).

Before our evening was over, we practiced the moves that were necessary to make the jump a success. After several practice sessions, it was clear that everyone understood their roles and responsibilities, so we patted one another on the backs and went our different ways.

I decided to go back to my table and get something to eat. As I sat down, a group of old friends joined me for an early dinner. It was great talking to everyone again; however, they brought this girl with them who, I must say, about drove me crazy. She had to be the filthiest person I had ever met in my life, both inside and out. Her name was Mary Merits, and all she ever wanted to do was talk about how great she was. If she saw anything about you that was unique, she was quick to point it out and belittle you in front of everyone—I have to admit that she was good at it. Just so you know, it looked like she hadn't taken a bath in months, smelt like it also; every other word that came out of her mouth was a curse word; and to top it all off, she was missing some teeth. I suspect she was hooked on crack or something. What a poor excuse for a human being. I was ashamed just being seen standing by her let alone having to admit I actually knew her. Fortunately, my childhood friend Jimmy asked me to go for a quick jump with him, and I exited the situation with a great sense of relief.

As I put on my gear in preparation for my jump with Jimmy, someone came by and said, "Don't jump out of that Beechcraft airplane over there. The owner just bought it for $10,000, and the person that usually mows the lawn was working on it this afternoon."

I have to admit I didn't believe him, so Jimmy and I signed up as two of the first skydivers to jump out of the Beechcraft. What drew me to the Beechcraft was the whole side of the plane was off, which made it easy and enjoyable to jump from.

There were twenty-some skydivers who signed up and paid to jump from the old Beechcraft airplane. I was the first in line, and Jimmy was right behind me. I must say I was shocked when they started the plane, and it blew out so much smoke that I couldn't see my way to the entrance. With some direction from Jimmy, I was able to find the entry, and we took our place in the airplane. I sat right behind the pilot and was surprised to see how sophisticated the old plane still looked with all its many gauges on the instrument panel. Eventually, all the paid passengers and the pilot boarded the plane, and off we went.

As we began to move forward, all the skydivers, except me, of course, started singing the skydiver song "You Picked a Fine Time to Fail Me, Reserve." I always thought skydivers were a little crazy, but when I heard them singing songs like that, it left me with little room for doubt. It didn't take long before we were accelerating down the runway, and that is when I noticed the pilot was thumbing through a book titled *How to Fly a Beechcraft*. In that moment, I thought to myself, *Don't you belong in the back of the plane?*

As we got up to speed, the pilot pulled back on the control column, and I could feel the old plane creak as it lifted off the runway. We must have gotten off the ground about ten feet when both motors backfired in unison, sending big black balls of smoke mixed with an occasional flame out the exhaust and forcing us to fall back to the runway. I was surprised that we didn't experience a more violent hit, but instead it just compressed the landing gear and we bounced back off the runway. In some ways it was a rather graceful bounce, and I got the feeling I was riding on the back of a giant jackrabbit as we bounced down the runway. The last bounce was at the end of the runway where there was a big circle of asphalt, which symbolized the ending point of the runway. We made the final bounce off the circle and then started falling into a field full of tall weeds. The next thing I knew we were cutting weeds with the props as the plain groaned to find strength for the miracle of flight. Eventually, the plane found the needed strength, and we were up and flying. In hindsight, it amazed me that the people in the back of the plane didn't miss a note during the whole ordeal. In fact, no one was aware of what I had just witnessed. I swept the sweat from my brow and turned around and started performing last-minute procedures in preparation for the impending jump with Jimmy.

Jimmy and I were the last ones out of the plane, and I must admit, it was worth the wait. It was a beautiful sight, standing on the edge of the old Beechcraft with thirteen thousand feet of jumping space between us and the desert floor. Our jump got off to a less than perfect start, as Jimmy left the plane before I was ready, and by the time I got out of the plane, Jimmy had an approximate one-thousand-foot head start on me.

As I jumped out of the old Beechcraft, I felt much safer skydiving than I did in the old rust bucket that I just escaped. I was often asked by people, "Why would you ever jump out of a perfectly good airplane?"

My response was always, "I never have."

In exiting the plane, I spent too much time focusing on Jimmy. As a result, I tumbled several hundred feet out of the plane. Once I got my wits about me, I arched my back, which allowed me to get in a stable falling position. Arching your back puts your center of gravity low enough to allow you to fall face forward toward the surface of the earth in a very stable manner. After I found myself in a stable falling position, I started looking down to see if I could locate Jimmy. I was shocked when I realized he was so far below me that he was a small dark dot in the sky below. I inherently knew what I needed to do next if I was to catch up with Jimmy.

Just to give you a little background: when you are in a stable falling position, you fall at approximately 120 miles per hour, but if you de-arch your back just the right amount, you will fall headfirst toward the surface of the earth. Because falling headfirst reduces the frontal area of the skydiver, you can accelerate up to speeds approaching 200 miles per hour. If you jump in the cold winter air of the Rocky Mountains and approach the 200-mile-per-hour terminal velocity, people on the ground can hear the crackling sound of your body as it speeds through the cold, dense air. It is one of those situations where you need to dress right, or you could easily and quickly get frostbite. Not that I would ever admit to doing such a thing—but just so you know.

In an effort to catch up with Jimmy, I de-arched my back and began my headfirst descent. I could feel my clothes violently clapping against my body as I approached the 200-mile-per-hour terminal velocity. In an effort to scratch out a little more speed, I de-arched just a little bit more and quickly realized my lust for more speed was too much, and I began tumbling through the air. For me, this was not a big deal as I knew from past experience that all I needed to do was arch my back and I would once again be in a stable falling position. After arching my back, I could feel the deceleration as I started slowing back down to the 120-mile-per-hour terminal velocity. The aggressive deceleration was throwing my body around somewhat violently, and the energy change between the two terminal velocities thrust my body forward (horizontal to the surface of the earth) at approximately 30 miles per hour.

At that point, I was falling at 120 miles per hour and moving forward at approximately 30 miles per hour. After a short period of time, everything stabilized, and I quickly spun around in hopes of finding Jimmy nearby. To my displeasure, Jimmy was nowhere to be found, so I looked below me. Although I was able to spot a small airplane flying way below me, Jimmy was nowhere to be found. Finally I thought to look above me, and there was Jimmy—a small dot in the sky above me. That's when I realized I had really messed up the jump. There was no longer enough space between me and the earth for Jimmy to catch up with me and do our relative work, so I went into a headfirst dive and pulled out so I could fly toward the airport in an effort to minimize my walking distance back to the tent community. This action would also ensure that Jimmy had plenty of deployment space without worrying about running into me. After reaching the planned deployment altitude of three thousand feet, I reached for the deployment chute and threw it out into the airstream, which, after deploying, had plenty of energy to pull out my main chute. After the deceleration from main deployment was complete, I checked out my parachute to make sure the deployment was fully successful. Fortunately it was, and I steered my way toward my destination.

I landed approximately one hundred yards from the edge of the tent community. Once safely on the ground, I turned around and started rolling up my parachute when out of the sky came Jimmy under his fully deployed chute. He was laughing about something, but he was too far away for me to effectively understand what was so comical. After he reached the ground, he came over to me and said, "Dude, you came tumbling past me in the air like I was standing still. Dude, you are so crazy."

I thought Jimmy knew better than to call me crazy—those were fighting words to me. I could feel my fists spontaneously prepare for a fight, but then I remembered this was my best friend. And besides that, when I went tumbling past him, I put him in a very dangerous situation that could have cost him his life. Plus, Jimmy quickly responded back and said, "Come on. You know I was just kidding around with you." Jimmy knew that was my hot button. People had called me crazy most of my life, and I didn't agree with it. To me, people thought I was crazy purely by association, and I didn't feel their judgments were at all fair. With those thoughts and words, I quickly felt a sense of civility come over me, and we walked back to camp while enjoying the moment together.

Once we arrived back at the tent community, we spread our parachutes out and began the labor-intensive task of repacking them. As we finished packing our chutes, Jimmy mentioned he had some things to do and would not be able to participate in the last jump opportunity of the evening. We agreed to meet for breakfast the next morning and went our separate ways.

After Jimmy left, I threw my diving gear over my back and started heading back to my campsite when I heard someone call out my name. I turned around, and to my surprise, it was Jesse. Jesse said, "Hey, John, come and join me for the last jump of the evening."

I felt extremely impressed that Jesse would ask me to jump with someone of his caliber. To be honest with you, I really enjoyed skydiving, but I was not overly talented at it. My last jump with Jimmy was fairly representative of my talent level. Now Jimmy, he was another story altogether. I could see Jimmy jumping with Jesse.

It's funny how we all have our strengths and weaknesses. Now racing stock cars on the dirt track, that was something else—that is where my talents were. I could beat Jimmy ten out of ten times on the track, just like he could beat me in the skies. With that in mind, I went over to Jesse and told him that I was in a way lower league than he was when it came to the skydiving world and that he would probably be better off jumping with someone nearer his caliber of talent.

Jesse said, "Don't be silly. Come follow me, and I will show you everything you need to know."

With that, I agreed to perform a jump with Jesse. I still couldn't figure out what it was about this guy. He was definitely someone special—someone like I had never met before, but I couldn't put my finger on it. Suffice it to say that when I was around him, I really felt I could rise above it all.

Of all the planes available to the skydivers, Jesse and I ended up on the rust-bucket Beechcraft that I had flown in earlier that day. I must admit I was pleasantly surprised that it behaved much better on the second flight. On our way up to jump altitude, Jesse started to teach me how to be more effective at performing relative work. He explained the techniques in a way that I hadn't heard them before, and I was surprised how well I understood what he taught me. Earlier on I heard someone call him the master teacher of skydiving, and now I knew why. Directly after my training was complete, a bell rang out letting us know that we had just reached jump altitude, which for this particular jump was ten thousand feet. It would give us just under one minute of free-fall time.

As we approached the edge of the Beechcraft where we would soon exit the plane, I could hardly believe how beautiful the desert sunset was. I had never seen the sun look so big, and the bronze sky was just breathtaking. The whole experience seemed so peaceful even in the midst of the chaos that is always there when you jump out of a plane speeding through the air at approximately one hundred miles per hour. My thoughts were brought back to reality as Jesse patted me on the back and started the countdown for exiting the plane.

At Jesse's signal, we both jumped out of the plane with perfect timing. I had never experienced such perfection. Once we had exited the plane, we started our planned routine, and I was able to implement everything he had taught me. After we clasped hands, he gave the signal, and we both made a 360-degree rotation and clasped hands again. Our timing was once again perfect. We performed several other moves, which were some of the more difficult moves I had ever been asked to perform. Although I did not do them perfectly, he did, and that made up for my shortcomings. Our last move before deployment was to do a backflip, come out facing each other, and once again clasp hands.

We pulled that last move off near perfection, and then per the original plan, Jesse waved his hands over his head to symbolize it was time for deployment. At this time, we both made a 180-degree turn to create separation between us and then deployed. After deployment, I looked around again and realized that the sunset was now even more beautiful than it had been during the exit from the plane. I turned my canopy toward my intended destination and then just soaked up the moment. I knew that evening would be one of the most memorable of my life. My landing was as peaceful as the evening. Once on the ground,

I rolled up my parachute and headed back to my campsite. I wasn't certain where Jesse had gone. I wanted to thank him for the experience, but I knew I would most likely see him the next day and could deliver my sentiments at that time.

I had a restful night and woke up to a beautiful Saturday morning. I could hear the airplanes warming up and smell the distinct odor that comes from burning high-octane aviation fuel. I also recognized the sound of skydivers getting ready for their morning jumps. The skydivers had all planned jumps with their relative work teams. They would get together and run through a dress rehearsal on what they hoped to do. Some teams would attempt to create the shape of a star, and others would choose to create a circle or some other geometrical shape that they chose.

At the end of this Easter Boogie, for the grand finale if you will, they were scheduling a jump with a goal of one hundred skydivers forming a huge circle in the sky. The interesting part of such an endeavor is none of the individual planes can carry one hundred skydivers, so they were going to have to take five or six planes up and coordinate the jump accordingly. Suffice it to say that these big jumps are seldom successful, as there is always going to be some lower-skilled skydivers who will not be able to close their part of the circle. With that being said, it can still be a lot fun watching everyone try, and if they were ever successful in closing the large circle, it would be a memory as well as a post jump party for the memory book.

As I mentioned earlier, I did not consider myself a great skydiver, so I had already decided that I would do everyone a favor and sit that one out. Of course, Jimmy was the type of skydiver who could successfully participate in such an event, and I made sure he signed himself up to participate in the grand finale that was scheduled to take place on Easter Sunday.

After cleaning up in the public restroom, at least the best you can clean up in a public restroom, I found my skydiving group, and we began practicing our jump. Jimmy was our lead skydiver, and he created a rather challenging formation, a formation that was most likely above my skill grade, but if he was all right with it, then I was all right with it. After a few ground practices, we were ready to try it at the twelve-thousand-foot level. We were allowed one practice jump, and then we would get a second jump that would be scored by the judges. The top three teams from the boogie would stand on a podium and receive cash prizes. The way they judged the jumps is a master skydiver would jump out with the group being judged and hover over them while filming the event with a small video camera attached to their helmet. The video was relayed live to the ground and reflected onto a jumbo screen for everyone to see, including the judges. The judges would score the jump based on standard criteria developed by the administrators of the boogie.

After eating a late breakfast with Jimmy, we headed off with our team toward the airplane. We were fortunate in that we got the best plane available, and once we got onboard, it took very little time getting up to our jump altitude of twelve thousand feet. Our first jump went like most first jumps in that we had plenty to work on. I was happy with my performance. I practiced a lot of what Jesse had taught me the evening before.

After reaching the ground, our skydiving team gathered around the Jumbotron where we watched our jump, while Jimmy stood on the stage with his laser and pointed out what we did right and what we still needed to work on. After the initial coaching was over, Jimmy took us to our practice area where we rehearsed what we had learned from our first jump. I had participated in these competitions with Jimmy multiple times, but this time Jimmy was different. I could tell that he really believed we had a chance to win the competition. With that type of leadership, everyone focused on their part, and we didn't stop practicing until the plane was ready to take us up for our competitive jump. What made this jump even more special is Jesse was our jumpmaster. On our way up to jump altitude, Jimmy and Jesse kept reminding us of the critical elements of our jump. When the door opened, everyone had their game face on, and we performed the best jump I have ever participated in. It was not good enough for first place, but we did get on the podium for a third-place finish. Needless to say, that was a memorable day for Jimmy and me.

I wish I could say it was more memorable than what I would experience the next day, but our victory was but a shadow of a thought compared to what was about to take place in my life.

It all began on Sunday morning when I went to the Jumbotron to watch the grand finale of the Easter Boogie. As I approached the big screen, I noticed an older gentlemen sitting at one of the tables. As I approached him, it became quite obvious that it was Jesse's father. It was hard to believe how much they looked alike. I went over and sat by him and said, "You must be Jesse's father."

He laughed and jokingly responded, "How could you ever guess?"

I introduced myself, and he said, "Yes, I heard all about you. Jesse speaks highly of you."

Before thinking about what to say, I blurted out, "Jesse told you about me?"

The father said, "Yes. He said you have a great future in the sport of skydiving."

I responded with, "He obviously believes in me more than I believe in myself."

The father laughed and said, "Yes, he tends to be that way."

I asked Jesse's father what he did for a living, and he told me he was a surgeon at one of the local hospitals. I would usually feel a little out of place in such company, but like Jesse, his father put me at ease. About that time the ambulances pulled up, and one of the paramedics came over and started to talk with Jesse's father. From their conversation, I realized the paramedic's name was Peter and Jesse's father's name was Elam. They had obviously worked very closely together in the past. As they talked, they made me feel comfortable being with them. I was still trying to figure out what it was about these guys that made them so different. What made them seem so good, and what was it that made everyone feel so comfortable while around them? The answers to my questions would have to wait, as I noticed a lot of activity taking place on the Jumbotron. I left Peter and Elam's presence and stood up close and personal to the big screen. This was definitely some kind of a special perspective on what was about to take place.

You may recall that the finale included approximately one hundred jumpers jumping from five planes in an effort to create a giant circle in the sky. No one had ever been able to pull this off in the past. This was a world-record attempt. Of course, it would be filmed by the master jumpers and shown live on the Jumbotron. From the Jumbotron, I was given the opportunity to see the jump from beginning to end from a very privileged perspective. I witnessed the excitement of everyone practicing the grand finale on the ground and then watching everyone board the planes and take off into the beautiful, bronze Arizona sky. Everything was going according to plan.

I thought to myself, *Could this finally be the year that they are able to pull this all together and break the record?!* With all the confidence I was witnessing, I started to believe that this could actually happen. I started doubting that thought when I noticed Mary Merits had joined the effort, and of course, she had to get on the same plane Jimmy was on. I thought to myself, *What a waste.*

It didn't take long before the planes were off the ground and up to jump altitude. I could see Jesse giving the pilot final corrections. Once the corrections were made, Jesse gave the sign for the group to get out of the plane. Everyone, including Mary, had an excellent exit out of the plane. From what I could tell, the jumpers from the other planes were equally successful. Jesse gave the group about a one-second head start before jumping out about fifty feet above them and videotaping the world-record attempt.

After the first thousand feet or so of free fall, the groups started coming together just as they had planned. From my perspective, things were going very well—that is, until I realized Mary Merits was nowhere in the picture. Jimmy was performing as I had expected, nearly perfect, until, like a flash, Mary Merits came blasting into the picture with a thirty-mile-per-hour horizontal speed and hit Jimmy directly in the rib cage. As a result of the collision, they went tumbling through the sky away from the rest of the jumpers.

Jesse realized, as did I, that the game had all of a sudden changed from a record attempt to trying to save lives. Jesse quickly chased after the two jumpers as they tumbled through the air. As the tumbling slowed, it appeared that both of them were knocked unconscious from the violent collision. Each of the skydivers had blood streaming from their mouths, and seconds after the accident, neither one of them showed any signs of life. Jesse was looking at both skydivers and trying to decide which one needed his help the most. About that time Jimmy woke up, arched, and started to create a controlled dive. That is all Jesse needed to see as he zeroed in on Mary in an attempt to save her before it was too late.

Jesse's first attempt at docking with Mary and deploying her parachute was unsuccessful. He shot directly underneath her. Things were now at a very critical stage, as they were running out of altitude, and another attempt to save Mary's life, in my opinion, was suicide. To my dismay, Jesse did not see it the same way, and he went in for another save. His second attempt was successful as he docked onto her limp body, pulled her into a position that would allow deployment, and deployed her chute. As soon as he did that, he quickly looked toward the ground to judge his altitude. I could tell by the ground rush that he had put off his deployment for too long. Jesse was going to die. Jesse realized it also and didn't even attempt a deployment. Instead, he turned his back to the ground so he could see if Mary's deployment was successful. He was basically looking to see if his death was going to be in vain. I can tell you that the last thing Jesse saw was a clean deployment of Mary's canopy.

I started screaming as I saw this selfless person crash right into the ground. The impact was probably about twenty yards from where I was standing, and I witnessed why skydivers call it bouncing. Suffice it to say that Jesse died a very violent death. I actually felt the ground shake as he hit the ground at approximately 130 miles per hour. After experiencing so much horror in such a short period of time, I could not stop screaming. I remember thinking to myself, *Would someone please wake me up from this terrible nightmare?* But no one could, because it was not a nightmare; it was reality.

As the dust started clearing, I could see the lights flashing from the ambulance as it drove over toward where Jesse had hit the ground. They were not trying to save Jesse; everyone knew that Jesse was dead. Everyone was now trying to save Jimmy and Mary Merits. I saw Jimmy coming down under a full canopy; he was conscious, but he was covered in blood. The ambulance crew was waiting for him as he landed his parachute like only Jimmy could. Jimmy told me he thought he was going to be all right.

That was when Peter called out to me. Peter was in the other ambulance, and they were giving Mary Merits mouth-to-mouth resuscitation in an effort to bring her back from the dead.

Peter looked at me and said, "John, you have got to go get Elam and tell him Mary is going to die if he doesn't help us."

At that point, everything was moving in slow motion. In hindsight, I realize that all the events were so overwhelming to me that I was in shock. I was walking around like a zombie.

I did as Peter said and walked away from the ambulance crews in search of Elam. As I did, the story only got worse as I looked over where Jesse hit the ground. His mother was there kneeling down on the ground and screaming. I won't tell you what I saw. Trust me; you don't want to know.

After walking for some time, I found Elam out in a field lying down in the fetal position sobbing like I had never seen anyone sob before. I hope to never witness it again. I thought to myself, *How can this damn story get any worse?* That is when I realized I had to get a grip on myself, or someone else was going to die. With that thought, I reached out and touched Elam on the shoulder and said, "Elam, if you don't come over and help Peter save Mary's life, she is going to die." Then I paused a second and quietly told him, "If you don't come and help, Jesse's death is going to be in vain." I then stood up and stepped back, realizing that I had done all that I knew how to do. No one could blame Elam for not coming to help after everything he had just been through.

I was somewhat surprised when he got up on his hands and knees and then slowly stood up. He wiped his eyes off and told me he was going to need my help and asked me to follow him. I did as I was told and followed Elam back to the ambulance. It was obvious he was an experienced surgeon, as he was able to turn off his emotions and turn his complete focus on the job at hand—saving people.

As we approached the ambulance, Peter began to brief Elam on the current state of the situation concerning Mary. By this time, Mary had already been placed on the stretcher inside the ambulance. She was also hooked up to all the machines. Elam pointed at a seat that was up by Mary's head and asked me to take a seat. He told me he would need me to cut some tubing as he instructed me to do so. I told him I would do my best, although inside I didn't know if I was going to be capable of helping Elam, as I had no experience performing such a task. But like Jesse, his father had a way about him that put me at ease.

Once everyone was settled into their proper locations, Elam started making strategic cuts into the side of Mary's rib cage. He started asking me to cut tubing to lengths defined by him with the surgical knife that was given me. I performed the tasks assigned me. I was not sure of everything that was going on, but it appeared to me that Elam was draining fluids from Mary's lungs. For the most part, it looked like blood. By the time the ambulance made it to the hospital, Mary appeared to be stabilized but never gained consciousness. When the ambulance stopped, a group of well-organized medical professionals pulled Mary out of the ambulance. Elam walked next to Mary's stretcher as the medical team rushed her into the surgery room.

It quickly became obvious that my job was finished, as everyone left me behind. I found a seat in the emergency room and just held my head in my hands as I reflected on all the events that had just taken place. I suspect I sat there for several hours trying to comprehend the incomprehensible. During this time, Mary and Elam were in surgery. I found out later that it took approximately seven hours of surgery to put Mary all back together again.

I finally made my way to the front desk of the hospital where I asked for Jimmy's room number. By this time, it was too late for visitors, but after looking me over, the attendant let me sneak through. Once in Jimmy's room, I noticed he was hooked up to a lot of machines and seemed to be in a deep sleep—at least that was my hope. At that point I was so tired that I just curled up in a ball and fell asleep on the floor next to his bed.

Approximately six hours later, I was awoken by Jimmy's nurse. After she performed all her tasks, I asked her Jimmy's prognosis. She told me that he seemed to be a pretty tough kid and the doctor thought he would recover just fine, but he was going to have to take it easy for a while. It felt so good to get some good news for a change. Shortly after that conversation, Jimmy woke up and asked me what was going down. I told him about his prognosis, and then I told him about everything I had seen from the perspective of the Jumbotron. I could tell he felt really bad about Jesse and was also concerned with Mary.

After the accident, something happened with everyone's perception of Mary. Before the accident, people were always rather skeptical of her, but after Jesse died for her, everyone put a very high value on her life. I was one of those people. After the accident, her life became extremely valuable to me, in part because I realized how much Jesse valued her life, and in part because I did not want Jesse's sacrifice to be in vain.

When things settled down, I asked Jimmy if he would like me to contact his family. He said, "Sure, but tell them I will be all right and will be home in no time."

You must understand that Jimmy comes from a very unique family. The first time I met them was after Jimmy invited me over to his home and they invited me to stay for dinner, which I did. During dinner, Jimmy's brother started talking about the fight he'd gotten into at the local bar the night before and how he really worked the guy over and then bit his nose off and spit it in his face. Everyone was laughing and patting one another on the back when they noticed I was at the end of the table in what they perceived was a mild state of shock. That is when Jimmy's brother looked over at me and asked, "Are you all right, John? You look like you have just seen a ghost."

I told them I was all right but was just thinking that I needed to keep my nose clean when I was around them. Everyone laughed, and from that day forward, I had become part of their family. I always knew if I ever needed help, I could count on them to back me up.

I called up Jimmy's family and told them what had happened. All his roughneck brothers told him to take it easy for a few days and noted that they'd save a cold one for him. Then they gave the phone to his mother, and she was a little bit more normal in her response to the situation and asked if she could talk with him. I handed the phone over to Jimmy, and he had a rather personal conversation with his mother in an effort to put her at ease. I remember thinking to myself, *Thank God for mothers.*

Later that day I went down to Mary's hospital room, but they wouldn't let anyone in because of the high risk of her getting an infection. I talked to the nurse who told me that Mary was in very critical condition and they still didn't know if she would make it. She told me Dr. Elam had done an exceptional job in surgery, and now it just depended on how strongly Mary desired to live. The nurse told me the best we could hope for would be an approximate one-month hospital stay with many more months of physical therapy afterward. The good news was that she was not paralyzed.

I stayed at the hospital for a few days until they released Jimmy. After Jimmy was released, we were leaving the hospital when I came across Elam. I immediately told him how sorry I was about Jesse. He started to lose his composure but quickly brought it back. He told me it had been a very difficult time for him and his family, but in the end, it would make everyone closer and everything would be all right. He noted that the memory of Jesse would never leave them. Elam then asked if Jimmy and I would come to Jesse's funeral and be pallbearers. Of course I accepted the invitation to help out but told him I didn't know if Jimmy would be able to lift anything by that time. He told me it wasn't a problem. Jimmy could walk beside me during the ceremony.

In our involvement in high-risk sports, both Jimmy and I had seen people die before, but we never went to their funerals, as we didn't understand the purpose of such an event. We knew they lived with a passion for life, and that memory was better than what we would get from a funeral. To be honest with you, we were both humbled to learn that someone would ask us to participate in his son's funeral. Before the funeral, both Jimmy and I went out and got a haircut and rented a suit for the funeral. The people who rented us the suits tried to teach us how to tie a tie, but eventually, they realized there was no hope. They instead tied them for us and told us to slip them over our heads and tighten them up before the funeral. I must say, by the time the funeral came around, we looked pretty civilized. We represented Jesse well as two of his pallbearers.

The funeral was different from what I was expecting. Instead of being an event that made everyone sad, it was an event celebrating a life well lived. I know I have mentioned it before, but I must note it again. There was just something different about Jesse and his family. When I say they were different, I mean it in a very good way. It makes me want to be more like them, for I have never met happier people. I must confess that I never felt I deserved such friends—that is, until I got around them, and then they made me feel like I really belonged. I have never been as happy as when I was around Jesse and his family. I remember before the funeral that I saw Elam tying his tie, and the simple act of watching him do that made me want to learn how to tie a tie. I wanted desperately to be like them. Just for the record, I must tell you that it was a painful experience, but I did eventually learn how to tie a tie.

After the funeral, Jimmy and I snuck away, as we felt that was a time for family only. Jimmy and I didn't say too much to each other that night, but somehow we both realized that our lives would never be the same after the experiences we'd had over the past few days. Jimmy was asked by his doctor to have a checkup three weeks after he left for home. As a result, we stayed at the tent community while he went through the healing process. On the day of his checkup, we went to the hospital and visited Mary. Mary was still rather weak but told us she would be getting out of the hospital in three more days and asked us if we wouldn't mind taking her to Jesse's grave site so she could spend some time there thanking him for her life and his sacrifice for her life. She told us she was going to live a better life, because she wanted Jesse to be proud of whom she had become.

After visiting with Mary, we agreed to hang around a few more days so we could take her to visit Jesse's grave site. That meant we would have to spend a few more days in the dreadful tent community, but we couldn't allow ourselves to turn down Mary's request. After visiting with Mary, we went down to Jimmy's doctor appointment. His appointment was scheduled to last for about four hours.

While I was in the waiting room, I was pleasantly surprised when Elam came by and visited with me. He sat down and asked me how everyone was doing. I gave him an update, and he was about to leave when I asked him to sit down for just a minute longer as I had something important to ask him. When he sat down, I could feel tears well up in my eyes and run down my cheeks as I asked him what made him and his family so unique.

He could sense my sincerity and spent the next three hours teaching me about phase 1, phase 2, and phase 3 behaviors. He told me that his family was unique in that they always tried to be phase 3 people. He told me Jesse was a very unique child in that he was phase 3 from the day he was born until the day that he died. Elam said Jesse was a very special son, and when he saw those skydivers in trouble, he immediately knew Jesse was going to sacrifice his life. Elam then asked me to do something that would forever change my life. Elam asked me to go teach everyone I could about phase 3 behavior and how to rise above it all. I told him that he could certainly find someone more refined and talented than myself to teach such important principles. He only responded with a smile.

From that point on, the direction of my life changed forever. I have since lectured all over the world about rising above it all. I also wrote a book—it is the one you are currently reading. It's all been in an effort to show Elam that he somehow picked the right person. I can only hope that he is not disappointed in my efforts.

After a few more days in the tent community, Jimmy and I took Mary to Jesse's grave site. On our way there, Mary asked us to drop her off near the grave site and then leave so she could spend some time there alone. She said she would call someone to pick her up when she was ready to leave. Jimmy checked her cell phone to make sure it was charged, and then we agreed to do as she requested. Rumor has it that something wonderful happened when Mary visited the grave site, but that is not my story to tell.

Jimmy and I drove back home, and Jimmy eventually recovered from all his injuries. Many years later I got a call from one of Jimmy's brothers who said he had died while performing a base jump off the Snake River Bridge located in a town called Twin Falls, Idaho.

After dropping Mary off, I did not see her until twenty-some years later. While in the Phoenix area on a business trip, I looked her up. It was so good to see her. After the accident, she stopped her drug use and eventually married this wonderful man, at least that is what she told me, and raised four boys of her own. It was an honor for me to meet her family. I cannot describe the joy I felt when I realized Mary's family was just like Elam's family. She had taught them in both word and deed about the nature of phase 3 behavior.

After visiting with Mary and her family I went to the hospital in hopes of finding Elam. The people at the hospital had never heard of a surgeon by the name of Elam. I had them dig deep into their records with the hope that I could get some contact information, but none existed. Elam, it turns out for me, is a rather elusive figure, but if this book should somehow find him, I would like him to know one thing. Thank you for your son.

And now I must end this story. I began this story like all great stories begin, and I will end it like all great stories end … and they lived happily ever after.

One of the lessons I hope you have learned from this story is that you will see greater value in your life as you begin to understand the sacrifices that have been made for your life. The sacrifices that have been made for your life started at the beginning of human history. People like Jesse literally sacrificed their lives, so you could experience the opportunities that you have today. So come to a fuller understanding of those sacrifices and start living your life with a new conviction of the value of this opportunity we refer to as life.

Chapter Seven

Hope versus Fear

Faith is like a seed that is planted in the ground. Initially, faith is just a thought with no evidence of that thought being true or untrue. Faith is powerful enough to motivate individuals to experiment with a given thought. If you experiment with thought and the thought is untrue, then the seed will die. If you experiment with thought and you find the thought to be true, then the seed evolves into a living, breathing plant. Just as the seed evolves to a plant, faith evolves into hope. Hope is a real power that is capable of changing human civilization, and lack of hope is capable of destroying human civilization. Without hope, you will never be capable of changing anything, including yourself. If happiness is the fuel that drives human nature toward evolving to phase 3 behavior, then hope is what ignites that happiness. Happiness does not exist without hope, and as a result, phase 3 does not exist without hope.

There is no such thing as a fulfilling and purpose-filled life without the critical element of hope. The best way I know how to explain the essence of hope is that it is the opposite of fear. Phase 3 is not and cannot be motivated by fear. Earlier in this book, I mentioned that courage is not the lack of fear but the ability to not let fear serve as our motivator. Hope goes beyond courage, and in its ultimate and purest form, it frees us from fear altogether.

Truth is like the sun is to the seed. Truth is what nourishes faith to become hope. If you know truth, the truth will set you free from fear. Hope is the most important element in living a fulfilling and productive life. It is the most important element that allows us to become what we are ultimately supposed to become. Without hope, there is no action. We cannot generate happiness without action. It takes action to evolve to phase 3.

In our earlier discussions, we learned about the nature of human nature by explaining phase 1, phase 2, and phase 3 behavior. We described happiness as the fuel that propels human nature to increasing levels of human evolution (phase 1, phase 2, and phase 3). Hope in its embryotic state is nothing more than a thought. Taking a thought and considering its logical merits (truth) is referred to as pondering (experimenting in one's mind). Pondering upon thought, assuming the thought has logical merit or truth, will eventually forge the thought into something more powerful. This more powerful thought is something I refer to as hope. What was once a thought now becomes powerful enough to promote action. Hope is the catalyst for action.

Without hope, there is no action, and where there is no action, you have no fulfillment, happiness, nor joy. For example, you may have read about phase 3 behavior and thought that it may be an idea worthy of your consideration. You ponder upon that thought until eventually the thought becomes powerful enough that you decide to take action and actually experiment with phase 3 behavior. After experimenting with a phase 3 activity, you come to the realization that you really do experience increased levels of happiness. What was once a thought and then a hope now becomes knowledge, and with increased experience, the knowledge becomes wisdom. Wisdom has the potential of serving the human race.

A by-product of hope is optimism. Tyrants, often referred to as control freaks, have a passionate hatred of optimism. Why, you may ask? Because optimism is too powerful for tyrants to control, and as a result, tyrants will do everything in their power to destroy optimism, which allows them to feel as if they have everyone under their control.

I once visited a country that was managed by a tyrannical government. My driver took me to various areas of the city, and I noticed everyone was just sitting around during what I considered to be part of the workday. I asked my driver why everyone was just sitting around doing nothing, and he told me they had no hope. I asked the driver what had happened to their hope. The driver told me that for a short period of time there was hope in the community, but it didn't last long. Of course, I asked him to tell me more.

He said, "See that man on the corner? His name is Joe, and he once started a construction company. It got so successful that he started buying dump trucks and other construction equipment. Joe would hire people from the local community to work for his company, and the whole community started to become hopeful of a better future and, as a result, industrious. Then one day the government started to fear Joe because of the hope, or power, he was creating in the community. They came in one morning and took all his equipment. That was the day hope died. That was the day everyone just sat around doing nothing."

Governments work best when they have to answer to ethical people. As soon as the governments no longer answer to ethical people, they will want to become more and more powerful, and they will attack anything that is seen to be more powerful than themselves, including hope and its by-product of optimism. Where there is hope, there is action, and where there is no hope, there is no action. You cannot have hope without action, and you will not observe action without hope.

If you are optimistic around a control freak, the control freak will become very pessimistic in an effort to destroy the optimistic environment. That way, that person can maintain the feeling of being in control of the situation and the people. It is an act of perversion. Tyranny will never create truly successful organizations. Tyrannical behavior is a by-product of matured and unadulterated phase I behavior.

In the beginning of this chapter, I wrote that hope is a real power. This begs the question that if hope is a real power, how powerful is it? Let me explain it this way. Our society has spent literally trillions of dollars with the hope of solving the curse of poverty. In doing so, the problem of poverty has not been solved. You may ask yourself why money doesn't solve the problem of poverty; after all, poverty is the lack of money. The answer to this problem is fundamentally simple. Poverty does not stem from the lack of money; money is not powerful enough to destroy poverty. Poverty comes from a lack of hope; only hope is powerful enough to solve the problem of poverty.

People who don't understand the fundamentals of hope have no business trying to solve the problem of poverty. You must understand the problem before you can effectively solve the problem. The only form of human behavior that has enough hope to effectively impact poverty is phase 3 behavior. One of the elements that makes phase 3 behavior so powerful is that it's full of hope, and hope has no fear. The natural by-product of a phase 3 community is that there will be no poor among them. You may ask yourself why there isn't poverty in a phase 3 community. The reason a phase 3 community will have no poor among them is because phase 3 behavior is capable of giving hope. In other words, the phase 3 community will solve poverty by giving hope.

Phase 2 behavior will try to solve poverty by giving money, because giving money will bring them popularity and popularity gives them power. Phase 2 behavior will try to solve poverty for its own glorification and is incapable of solving poverty for the impoverished.

I will end this chapter approximately the same way I started this chapter by noting that hope is a real power.

Chapter Eight

Closing Thoughts

Congratulations! You have made it to the final chapter. I hope you have found the journey both educational and inspirational. The objective of this chapter is to summarize the lessons learned and to add some final information that did not comfortably fit into other areas of the book. I am constantly pondering and expanding my thoughts concerning personal fulfillment, and in this chapter, I will publish my latest thoughts. These thoughts have not been tested over time like much of the information published in earlier chapters were during endless hours of lecturing and responses to mountains of student input in the form of end-of-lecture surveys. So welcome to the cutting edge of my current thoughts.

This book began with a discussion on the nature of human nature. The model rested on two basic assumptions, the first being that the mother of all motivators is survival. People will do amazing things just to survive. The second assumption was that every person must perceive he or she stands out in a crowd or that person will die. Because people do not want to die, they will figure out a way to stand out in a crowd.

The starting point of human behavior is referred to as phase I behavior. Phase I behavior tears people down to give the perception of standing out in a crowd. Phase I behavior will naturally identify uniqueness, amplify uniqueness, and then belittle uniqueness. Phase I behavior is referred to as the cheap drug of human behavior. Phase I behavior is motivated by fear and tends to solve problems using PBP. From the phase

I perspective, problems are solved effectively and efficiently using PBP. Outside the phase I perspective, you will see that phase I behavior causes more problems than it solves. Phase I behavior is inherently destructive and believes that winning battles is solving problems, even though after winning battles the organization's performance never improves. If you solve a problem in a phase I organization without a battle, then from the phase I perspective, you never actually solved a problem. Phase I behavior demands contention, and if contention is not there, then the feeling of moving forward will also be absent.

If you choose to live your life in phase I behavior, you will receive the fruits of phase I behavior, which include being envious, jealous, hateful, and easily offended. Phase I behavior is the birthplace of racism, sexism, and so on. Ultimately, phase I behavior will make you and people around you miserable. I would recommend that you rise above it all. In the act of rising above it all, you will have many critics say that you are not capable of rising above. If you are to rise above it all, you must teach yourself how to ignore negative criticism. Critics who offer up purely negative criticism do so for only one reason, and that is to gain control over people. However, they can only control you with criticism if you care what they think. In the end, it is up to you if you will give phase I behavior power to direct your life.

Remember that you must learn to ignore negative criticism if you are to rise above it all. People usually need help from others to rise above phase I behavior. To do this, you need to learn skills and talents. You may need help from others to gain these newfound skills and talents. Don't be motivated by your fears, or you will never rise above phase I behavior, because you can never become greater than that which motivates you. You will feel fear from time to time, but that does not mean you have to be motivated by it. The definition of courage is not the elimination of fear but the refusal to use it as a motive.

Phase 2 behavior takes place when people develop their skills and talents to such an extent that they can use them to stand out in a crowd. Standing out in a crowd by exercising one's skills and talents does not have the bitter aftertaste of phase I behavior. The primary force that evolves human nature to higher levels of behavior is the fact that higher levels of behavior feel better than the lower levels of behavior. People will spend a lifetime developing their skills and talents simply because at the end of the day they feel better about themselves.

Phase 2 behavior still has the stains of phase 1 behavior in that phase 2 behavior still desires to witness others failing. The difference is that phase 1 behavior desires everyone to fail, while phase 2 behavior only desires those who are developing skills and talents similar to its own to fail. Phase 2 behavior has a high respect for skills and talents. People in a phase 2 organization will not let you lead them unless they perceive you as more skilled and talented than they are. As soon as they perceive that they are more skilled and talented than their leader, the leader can no longer effectively lead the phase 2 organization. When phase 2 behavior does something of value, it will seek the well-deserved glory.

Remember that phase 2 behavior uses skills and talents to stand out in a crowd and cannot stand out in a crowd if it does not receive credit for what it does. In short, phase 2 behavior seeks after its own glory. I am not saying that phase 2 is bad; I am just stating it is the nature of human evolution. Remember that people are just trying to survive. Some people survive by tearing people down, while other people survive by exercising their skills and talents. Phase 2 behavior is more constructive than phase 1 behavior. Neither of these forms of behavior generates enough power to facilitate cultural change.

Phase 3 behavior is the crowning achievement of human behavior. Phase 3 behavior, applied correctly, has the power to change organizational culture. Phase 3 behavior seeks not its own glory but only desires to lift others up. Phase 3 behavior has the purest of motives and will never fail you. When acting out in phase 3 behavior, you will never look back and regret your behavior. To lead a phase 3 organization, you simply teach them constructive principles.

Phase 3 behavior will recognize correct principles and will use them for effective self-government. In a phase 3 organization, you can teach the members of the organization methodologies that will move society forward, and phase 3 will simply implement it. Phase 3 behavior does not desire recognition programs, and it does not respond to attempts to motivate by fear. Phase 3 behavior is only motivated by the opportunity to make things better. You cannot force phase 3 behavior, and attempting to do so is a moral perversion.

Sometimes people with lower levels of behavior will try to force phase 3 behavior for their own glorification. This will never work, because you can never raise an organization above your predominant level of behavior. In other words, use of phase 1 and phase 2 behaviors makes it impossible to create a phase 3 organization. You know you are ready to evolve to phase 3 behavior when phase 2 behavior becomes boring. When phase 2 behavior becomes boring, then phase 3 behavior will feel empowering and will help you reach new levels of fulfillment and productivity. You cannot reach phase 3 behavior without first mastering phase 2 behavior.

Phase 3 behavior demands sacrifice, and sacrifice demands character. Character is defined as the ability to follow through with a decision long after the emotions of making the decision are gone. When sacrifice meets emotion, emotions evaporate. When you perform a phase 3 event, emotions will disappear, and you must be able to follow through with the good deed even in the absence of emotion. If you cannot sacrifice, then you cannot perform phase 3 behavior. Sometimes phase 3 behavior has to sacrifice its own popularity to lift others up. Phase 3 behavior is capable of doing this because it does not desire to stand out in the crowd. Standing out in a crowd is no longer a necessity in life, as you have risen above it all. And why did you rise from phase 2 behavior to phase 3 behavior? Because it felt better. It is really quite simple. When you rise from one phase of behavior to another phase of behavior, it will most likely be lonely because that which you once had in common with your peer group you are no longer there, and they may not enjoy hanging out with you like they once did. Rising above it all can be a lonely endeavor, so you will ultimately have to decide what is more important to you. Many people do not evolve to higher levels of behavior because they don't want to leave their comfort zones. Rising above it all demands sacrifice, and sacrifice demands character.

Your capability to sustain higher levels of human behavior is only as strong as your character. When the sacrifices of phase 3 behavior exceed your level of character, you will slide down to lower levels of human behavior. If you will leave scratch marks all the way down the curve and after bottoming out you scratch all the way back to the top, then you will effectively increase your character. You cannot experience the rise without experiencing the fall.

Be aware that when you bottom out in lower levels of human behavior, phase 1 behavior will come out of the woodwork and try to convince you that because you're not perfect, you can no longer do perfect things. This is not true. Imperfect people can do perfect things. Phase 1 behavior will try to gain control of you through the art of negative criticism. Many people believe this negativity and never try again to regain the joys of phase 3 behavior. Remember that you do not have to be perfect to do perfect things, so pull yourself up and rise above it all.

Phase 1 behavior will try to convince you that your weaknesses are something to be ashamed of when, in reality, these supposed weaknesses are only potential strengths. A weakness should be seen as a blessing and not a curse. The only time a weakness becomes a curse is when you accept that it is a curse and make the mistake of believing that you cannot overcome the weakness. You will often hear people say, "But I was born that way." We all start out at phase 1 behavior, but we do not have to stay there, because human behavior is capable of evolution. Don't live life for what you are but live life for what you hope to become.

If you spend all your days trying to hide your weaknesses because of the I-Am-Great Cloud, then you will never overcome them and you will never evolve human nature. If you hide your weaknesses because you're afraid that people will make fun of them, then you will not evolve to higher levels of human behavior. You should not let critics dictate your life. Your life is to be lived on your terms and not on the terms of others. If you do not become the captain of your own ship, then you will never rise above it all. There are a lot of people out there who want to be the captain of your ship—don't let them. Everyone has the right to be the captain of his or her own ship—don't give the gift away. Phase 3 behavior is the by-product of people who are free to choose for themselves. You can become so independent that it can become difficult for people to live with you, so always remember the rule "moderation in all things." At the end of the day, do what you know to be right.

I will now provide one last thought concerning the nature of human nature and the three forms of human behavior. I will use the figure below to help explain my thoughts.

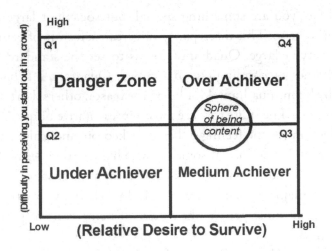

Notice that the figure above is drawn as two-dimensional. In other words, there are two variables used to describe the phenomena. The horizontal axis shows the relative desire to survive, and the vertical axis shows difficulty in perceiving you stand out in a crowd. The figure suggests that not everyone is born with the same desire to survive. The figure also suggests that each of us has a different perception on what it takes for us to feel that we are standing out in a crowd. You must remember that standing out in a crowd is only a perception. Some people wake up in the morning and look in the mirror, and that is all they need to feel that they stand out in a crowd. Other people have to shake the world to perceive that they stand out in a crowd.

Remember that these two variables were the two basic assumptions of the original model. You will notice that I took the space created by the two variables and broke it into four quadrants. Quadrant I is an individual who has a relatively low desire to survive; it is very difficult for individuals in this quadrant to feel they stand out in a crowd. Quadrant I tends to act out in self-destructive behavior. Quadrant I is not healthy and isn't a fun place to live.

Quadrant 2 is defined as a person who has a relatively low desire to survive but finds it relatively easy to perceive standing out in a crowd. This combination of attributes tends to make the individual an underachiever. The challenge with quadrant 2 is that your perception of standing out in a crowd does not match society's perception of standing out in a crowd.

You will feel you are something special, but society at large does not perceive it to be so. This discrepancy can create a feeling of being picked on by society at large. Quadrant 4 tends to set the standard for what society defines as standing out in a crowd. Quadrant 2 behaviors can potentially blame quadrant 4 for being the reason others don't recognize their greatness. The traits that are most representative of quadrant 2 are underachievement, the feeling of being picked on, and jealousy.

Quadrant 3 is defined as someone who has a strong desire to survive but perceives standing out in a crowd without a lot of sacrifice. I would suggest the majority of mature people live their lives with this low confidence. For most people, the sphere of being content partially lies in quadrant 3.

The sphere of being content or the sphere of contentment is where we feel at peace with ourselves and what we spend most of our time trying to find. The sphere of contentment will be slightly different for different people, but I would argue that it will have an overlap between quadrant 3 and quadrant 4. Note that I call it the sphere of being content even though it is drawn as a circle. This observation suggests there is another dimension to this model. We will discuss this later.

Quadrant 4 is defined as someone who has a strong desire to survive, but it is very difficult for this person to perceive standing out in a crowd. This quadrant is what creates overachieving behavior. As mentioned earlier, quadrant 4 is the behavior that defines, for society, what standing out in a crowd looks like. Quadrant 4 demands large levels of sacrifice and will ultimately demand the creation of character, more so than do the other quadrants.

The natural question then becomes, how do we move between quadrants? Obviously we are born with certain characteristics that put us at a given location within the quadrants. I would argue that inherently we may start out at a given location, but that does not mean we have to spend our entire lives there. I feel that environmental factors can also impact the quadrant. For example, you may find yourself in quadrant 2 and feel as if you are standing out in a crowd but that society doesn't see it. Therefore, you feel a little jealous and ultimately realize that your perception of standing out in a crowd needs to be recalibrated. The recalibration puts you into quadrant I, the danger zone. The danger zone is not a fun place to live, so you desire to find your sphere of contentment.

This desire will ultimately drive you to quadrants 3 and 4. Most individuals, but not all, tend to generate a greater desire to survive as they approach quadrants 3 and 4 because it is easier to want to survive as life becomes more rewarding. You have more to fight for. People who fight the hardest tend to be the people who feel they have the most to lose. This suggests that society at large will evolve toward higher levels of contentment. One of the reasons I gave the earlier assignment to perform a phase 3 event is because phase 3 events tend to migrate people to more constructive quadrants.

The model shown in this figure is two-dimensional. In my opinion, the reality is better modeled in three dimensions. The third dimension would be represented by a third axis that comes out of the page toward the reader (z-axis). The third dimension is the phase of behavior, or motives of behavior. The starting point of the three dimensions is the starting point of human nature, or what I called phase 1 behavior. As one travels up the z-axis from phase 1 to phase 2 and ultimately into phase 3, the nature of the two-dimensional relationship shown in the figure will change.

In the current figure, the sphere of being content is a cross section of a sphere. As people reach the sphere of being content, they will get a vision of greater contentment than what they currently have. If they continue to search for greater contentment, they will work their way up the third dimension. As they work their way up the third dimension, the circle on the current figure will grow progressively smaller until it no longer exists on the figure shown. This would suggest that the rules change as you evolve along the third dimension.

Phase 1 and phase 2 are limited in scope. You will rise above them as you progress, assuming you desire to do so. Phase 3 does not end. It is infinite in nature, and ultimately your desire to find greater contentment will lead you to greater spheres of contentment, and you will never come to a point where greater contentment cannot be discovered. This infinite journey is the ultimate goal in the evolution of human nature. This is why I wrote perfection is a journey, not a destiny.

There is another element of human behavior that I do not completely understand, but I do recognize its destructive nature. This is the destructive nature to believe negative lies more readily than believing positive truths. This element is what allows negative critics to be so powerful in our society. I'd like to tell you a story to illustrate. Once upon a time, there was a little boy who got abducted and asked his abductor, "Why are you taking me away from my home?"

And the abductor said to the little boy, "I am taking you away from your home because you left the gate open and the dog ran away, and as a result, your parents no longer love you and have asked me to take you away."

The little boy believed his abductor and felt very bad. The years went by, and eventually the cops found the abductor and returned the little boy to the police station where his parents were anxiously awaiting his arrival. When the little boy arrived at the police station, the parents fell to their knees and hugged the little boy. As you may imagine, the tears flowed freely. Then the little boy said to his parents, "I'm sorry I left the gate open and the dog got away, and I am really sorry that you don't love me anymore."

Hearing this from her son made the mother fall to the floor where she cried out in pain. The father said to his son, "How can you believe such an ugly, perverted lie? Don't you know that we love you more than anything in the whole universe? How could we possibly hate something that we have created?"

After the father spoke to his son, he embraced his son and wife in the hope that their love would heal the boy.

It is up to you to write the end of the story on whether the child ultimately believes his father or the abductor.

My experience suggests that people will believe the abductor before they will believe the father. I don't know why people will readily embrace a negative lie before they will embrace a positive truth. But that's human nature, and I suspect that we have to learn to work within the reality of the situation in which we find ourselves. The abductor telling the child he was not loved is what I refer to as the big lie. Believing the big lie is the most destructive element of human nature, even more destructive than the I-Am-Great Cloud.

You can only see the brutality of the big lie from the phase 3 perspective (the perspective of the parents). From the phase 1 and phase 2 perspectives, the big lie seems completely logical. I do not know why this is so, but maybe I will someday; however, that thought has not yet matured. I feel that it has something to do with the harshness of judgments that come from phase 1 and phase 2 behaviors, and in the harshness of these judgments are the only judgments with which we know how to judge ourselves. The discouragement that comes from phase 1 and phase 2 behaviors is largely self-inflicted. Suffice it to say that I find it to be very discouraging that people believe in the big lie. If I only had a magic wand and but one wish, I would use the wish to destroy the big lie.

I suspect believing the big lie has something to do with the nature of the human evolution. Phase 1 behavior will believe anything that is bad. For example, if you hear a rumor that the neighbor had an affair and the family is going to break up, phase 1 behavior would readily believe it and would get an adrenaline rush at the thought of telling everyone about it. Phase 1 behavior celebrates others' failures. Phase 1 will believe in truth as long as it represents something bad happening to someone else. Phase 2 behavior will believe the truth as long as it is popular, but if the truth is not popular, this person will be highly offended by the truth and try to destroy it. Phase 3 behavior will believe the truth, and the truth will set this person free. Phase 3 behavior will believe the father. Phase 3 behavior will see the beauty around, including the beauty in each and every person despite everybody's imperfections and perhaps even because of them. May we all be blessed enough to see the beauty in others.

Perhaps you have already come to the realization that I tried to make this book the magic wand. I fear it has fallen terribly short. However, if it will inspire one person to live a more fulfilling and productive life, then my sacrifice will be but a grain of sand on the large, beautiful beach of sacrifices we call life.

Remember that life is like a book, and you only get to write one of them. You are the only one authorized to write your book, so make it a great one! This is my only hope.

This is not the end but simply a new beginning, should you choose it to be.

Blue skies.

Thank you, iUniverse team and my dear friend

Fred Pingel

Printed in the United States
By Bookmasters